SO-ASX-565

NATIVES & SETTLERS

1017298650
342.710872 NAT

Natives & settlers, now &
then : historical issues an
KAMLOOPS LIBRARY

KAMLOOPS DEC 2 8 2007
LIBRARY

WELLS   DEC 16 1971
LIBRARY

NATIVES

NATIVES & SETTLERS · NOW & THEN
HISTORICAL ISSUES AND CURRENT PERSPECTIVES
ON TREATIES AND LAND CLAIMS IN CANADA

Edited by Paul W. DePasquale

& SETTLERS

 THE UNIVERSITY
of ALBERTA PRESS

CANADIAN REVIEW *of* COMPARATIVE LITERATURE
REVUE CANADIENNE *de* LITTÉRATRE COMPAREÉ

Thompson-Nicola Regional District
Library System
300-465 VICTORIA STREET
KAMLOOPS, BC   V2C 2A9

Published by
The University of Alberta Press
Ring House 2, Edmonton,
Alberta, Canada, T6G 2E1
&
*Canadian Review of Comparative
Literature/Revue Canadienne de Littératre
Compareé*
317 Arts Building, University of
Alberta,Edmonton, Alberta,
Canada, T6G 2E5

LIBRARY AND ARCHIVES OF CANADA
CATALOGUING IN PUBLICATION

Natives & settlers, now & then :
historical issues and current
perspectives on treaties and land claims
in Canada / edited by Paul Depasquale.

Co-published by: Canadian review
of comparative literature/Revue
canadienne de littérature comparée.
Includes index.

ISBN: 978-0-88864-462-6

1. Native peoples—Canada—Claims.
2. Native peoples—Canada—Treaties.
3. Native peoples—Canada—
   Government relations.
I. DePasquale, Paul W. (Paul Warren),
   1965-
II. Title: Natives and settlers, now and
   then.

KE7709.5.N385 2007
342.7108'72   C2007-901165-9

Copyediting by Leslie Robertson.
Cover & text design by Jason Dewinetz.

No part of this publication may be
produced, stored in a retrieval system,
or transmitted in any forms or by
any means, electronic, mechanical,
photocopying, recording, or otherwise,
without the prior written consent of
the copyright owner or a licence from
The Canadian Copyright Licensing
Agency (Access Copyright). For
an Access Copyright license, visit
www.accesscopyright.ca or call toll free:
1-800-893-5777.

NOTICE TO LIBRARIANS:
*Natives & Settlers, Now & Then: Historical
Issues and Current Perspectives on
Treaties and Land Claims in Canada*
is co-published with the Canadian
Review of Comparative Literature/
Revue Canadienne de Littérature
Compareé and is also Canadian Review
of Comparative Literature/Revue
Canadienne de Littérature Compareé
34.1 (2007) (ISSN: 0319-051X)

Copyright © *Canadian Review of
Comparative Literature/Revue Canadienne
de Littérature Compareé* 2007
Volume 34, no. 1 (2007)

ISSN: 0319-051X
ISBN 978-0-88864-462-6

LIBRARY AND ARCHIVES CANADA
CATALOGUING IN PUBLICATION

Printed and bound in Canada by
Kromar Printing Ltd.

First edition, first printing, 2007.
All rights reserved.

The University of Alberta Press is
committed to protecting our natural
environment. As part of our efforts,
this book is printed on Enviro Paper: it
contains 100% post-consumer recycled
fibres and is acid- and chlorine-free.

The University of Alberta Press
gratefully acknowledges the support
received for its publishing program
from The Canada Council for the Arts.
The University of Alberta Press also
gratefully acknowledges the financial
support of the Government of Canada
through the Book Publishing Industry
Development Program (BPIDP) and
from the Alberta Foundation for the
Arts for its publishing activities.

Canada Council   Conseil des Arts
for the Arts   du Canada

Canadä

Thompson-Nicola Regional District
Library System
300-465 VICTORIA STREET
KAMLOOPS, BC   V2C 2A9

1017298650

CONTENTS

FOREWORD

To WRITE SOMETHING in the pre-matter of this book is a privilege.
The editor and contributors have put together a collection that will make
a difference in many fields and places. Above all, this volume is a testament to the importance of Native Studies. The contributors each have key
stories to tell. And I will not add too much prefatory delay to those stories,
so that the reader can quickly get to the heart of the matter.

This volume grows out of a conference I proposed and whose framework I set up as part of a series of meetings examining Native-European
contacts. This is not the place to go into my family history and connection as a child with Native peoples; one instance from my time as an
undergraduate will suggest my involvement. From 1976 to 1977, I was
an interpreter and, in 1978, staff supervisor at Sainte-Marie-among-the-
Hurons, a reconstruction of a mission where the Hurons or Ouendat
and French met between 1639 and 1649, until it was destroyed by the
Iroquois in that year. As a scholar, I later helped to organize a number of
conferences and colloquia that involved or centred on Native peoples. In
1992, Richard Bauman, a law professor at the University of Alberta, and
I involved Native speakers at our conference "Explorations in Difference"
(later published under that title by University of Toronto Press). Anne
McLellan, then Associate Dean of Law at the University of Alberta, opened
the conference, and Sharon Venne, a contributor to *Natives and Settlers*,
was one of the participants. In 2000–2001, I organized a conference at
Princeton, where I was a Visiting Professor, in which all other Canadian
participants were Native. In keeping with this series of conferences involving or focusing on Native speakers and issues, I recently (in June
2006) organized a round-table involving members of Native Studies and

Comparative Literature to explore issues of aboriginal peoples inside and outside Canada (our guest speaker was Australian). Olive Dickason was a key part of another conference, and her work in the field has been an inspiration.

The genesis of this current project lay with the Medieval and Early Modern Institute (MEMI) at the University of Alberta, of which Glenn Burger and I were the founding co-directors. In keeping with the interests of the directors, the executive, and the members of the Institute, we developed two conferences. The first was "Making Contact" in 1998, which Glenn and I co-organized, from which a collection of essays was published by the University of Alberta Press. Paul DePasquale, the editor of this volume, was one of the participants and contributors. In 1999–2000, I thought that we should have another conference that included Natives and settlers, so I came up with an idea for one that bore the title of this book. This conference, rather than merely including Native issues, would actually focus on Natives and Native issues as the centre of the event. And they were, with great success. I wish to thank all those who participated in and supported the conference, some of whose work appears in this volume. One of the mandates of MEMI was to publish collections and disseminate research, as well as to bring students, faculty, and the community together in all their multiplicity. So I intended to produce a volume from the start as a co-publication with the *Canadian Review of Comparative Literature*, of which I am the editor. Glenn Burger and the MEMI executive supported this idea, as they had *Making Contact,* so MEMI deserves thanks for its financial support of both volumes. The University of Alberta Press has also supported both projects. Patricia Clements, Patricia Demers, and others have been key supporters of MEMI and, without their help in founding the Institute, it would have been difficult to have put together these conferences and subsequent publications. For these two books, Glenn Rollans, Linda Cameron, Mary Mahoney-Robson, Leslie Vermeer, Cathie Crooks, Alan Brownoff, Michael Luski, Peter Midgley, and others at the University of Alberta Press have been a pleasure to work with, and their care and talent are among the reasons I approached them with these publications. At some point in the process, I asked one of my graduate students, Paul DePasquale, now a professor at the University of Winnipeg, to become involved with the organization of the conference, and then thought it a good idea to hand the book project over to him. He has done a fine job bringing the contributions together into a book and so deserves thanks and gratitude.

But more important than the genesis is the outcome, this splendid collection. The contributors are an accomplished group who are leaders in their communities and fields. Paul DePasquale's Introduction gives some background to the meeting of various Native and settler groups from Jamestown in Virginia and beyond, especially in Canada, and most particularly in Winnipeg and Manitoba where DePasquale works and lives. The issues he raises, including those of land claims, are vital to the health and harmony of Canada's future; history is important partly because of its typology with the present. As he discusses the contributors' work, my comments will be brief.

Sharon Venne brings a Cree and indigenous point of view to treaty-making, to settlers' myths about treaties and reserves, and to the fact that even the lands around and under the University of Alberta, where the original "Natives and Settlers" conference was held, were aboriginal. In fact, as Venne points out, all of the Americas were indigenous lands. In her view, the only legal basis for sharing land in these places is a treaty. She brings an indigenous view to international law, and she tells an important side of the story. Treaties should not be about invasion and robbery. In standing up for Native treaty rights, Venne calls upon decisions in the House of Lords and the United Nations. In this creation, indigenous peoples will not be discounted in their own lands. Patricia Seed examines the case of English dispossession of Natives in territories that now lie within the United States, Canada, and New Zealand. Seed argues that indigenous peoples must seek their rights through treaties—the etymology of which term and its cognates she treats—under the framework set out for them by England. She reminds us that land law developed early in England, so when it came time to colonize, such law was well established. Colonial fictions are another concern of Seed's tale of English colonization, which she considers within a European context. Both oral and written treaties are crucial to her position, and she examines an example of a bilingual treaty with the Maori in New Zealand. For Seed, treaties in Canada should be considered as occupying a midpoint between those in the United States and New Zealand, and Seed's comparative work on treaties in all three countries is suggestive in many ways. She argues that states that were former Hispanic and English colonies have come to terms with that colonization and now seek decolonization. Frank Tough and Erin McGregor discuss a case from 1994, when the Métis of northwest Saskatchewan made a land claim against Canada and Saskatchewan and met important challenges. Tough and McGregor's study establishes a model of the land scrip system. By examining one individual scrip claimant's paper trail, they are able to illustrate the ways in which this system may have failed. More specifically, it failed to meet the standards of conventions for conveying property. This case study has implications well beyond itself, and the authors provide a detailed context for it. The scrip system, according to Tough and McGregor, raises basic questions about Métis and aboriginal title and how scrip coupons were employed in prairie land use and tenure. Tough and McGregor reconstruct a trail of documents that show that the scrip system was a strange attempt to bring together two views of property, an Indian title that had to be extinguished and a European system that had to be enforced (involving tenures, rights, and fee simple title). We are still living with this failure to mesh the two. Harold Cardinal brings the perspective of a Nihiyow or Cree to the conversation. He observes that the colonizing experience has shaped both the aboriginal and the white communities and says that he finds valuable Patricia Seed's reminder that there is a diversity of experience among Native peoples as well. Cardinal thinks that Natives should look at themselves both as individuals and as members of their communities, and should come to understand with clarity, honesty, and accuracy what is happening to them and in those communities. Moreover, Cardinal sees that, for both aboriginal and non-aboriginal peoples in Canada, like those elsewhere colonized by Europe, decolonization and nation building continue. He argues that decolonization requires the deconstruction of racist colonial paradigms, a centuries-old, state-sponsored system that was built to exercise a hold on the minds and souls of First Nations peoples in Canada. In his observations on theory and practice, Harold Cardinal calls for a new kind of comparative study of Aboriginal and Western peoples. "Questions" forms the penultimate section of this collection, and, rather than give any of these queries and responses away, I will only say that they invoke the openness and exchange of the conference itself, a kind of exemplary round-table. I remember listening with excitement to the exchange of ideas, and now I am glad to help to recreate this atmosphere in the book as Paul Depasquale has transcribed it. The final contribution is "Remembering Harold Cardinal," in which Paul DePasquale, Patricia Seed, Frank Tough, and Sharon Venne remember this remarkable leader. I would like to invoke his memory as well as to thank him for all he has done, as a leader and as a person, for his people and for Canada. It was an honour to have him speak at our conference and to read his words here in these pages.

And so this collection extends an invitation to think afresh about Natives and settlers in order that we might live together in renewed ways that show mutual respect. For settlers especially, it is important to familiarize themselves with the history and culture of Native peoples and to disassociate themselves from unspoken and unexamined assumptions that comprise a legacy too rarely characterized by mutuality. Canada is multicultural, so that this story is a many-sided one, in which all the peoples here and elsewhere must move forward with an awareness of the story of empires and colonies in order to forge something new and better, something fair, good, beautiful, and just.

Jonathan Hart
December 2006

EDITOR'S ACKNOWLEDGEMENTS

THANK YOU FIRST to Cathy Sewell (1962–2001), respected Aboriginal educator, singer, dancer, actor, writer, and role model. In 2000, Cathy attended the conference "Natives and Settlers Now and Then" at the University of Alberta and was the first to encourage this book by asking afterwards how soon a printed version would be available to read for those who couldn't attend. This publication is in honour of Cathy's courage, spirit, and commitment to Aboriginal peoples through her work at Aboriginal Student Services, University of Alberta, and beyond.

My thanks to Nancy Van Styvendale for transcribing the recordings of the original presentations, questions, and discussions; to Kelly Burns, for research assistance at various stages; and to Andrea Siemens, who transcribed my interview on treaty-making with Omushkego ("Swampy Cree") historian Louis Bird, which I cite in the introduction. I am grateful to Jonathan Hart, who encouraged this project and generously shared his knowledge and experience. The University of Minnesota Press gave permission to print Patricia Seed's work, part of which appears in *American Pentimento: The Pursuit of Riches and the Invention of "Indians"* (2001). Thank you to the anonymous readers of the manuscript, and to Anne Lindsay and James Sinclair, for suggestions on earlier drafts. Alethea Adair, Linda Cameron, Cathie Crooks, Peter Midgley, Mary Mahoney-Robson, and others at the University of Alberta Press gave efficient, professional assistance and much encouragement throughout. A warm thank you to Leslie Robertson for her careful eye and intelligent copyediting work on this project. Erin McGregor, researcher at the Métis Archival Project, helped with several digital images. The research used in my introduction was funded over the years by the Six Nations of the Grand River

Post Secondary Education Office, the Social Sciences and Humanities Research Council of Canada, and the Canada–U.S. Fulbright Program. My work on the project was completed with support from the University of Winnipeg, including a research leave in summer/fall 2006.

The book's progress was delayed somewhat by the illness and then, sadly, the passing, on June 3, 2005, of one of its contributors, Dr. Harold Cardinal, the day after he had received formal notification that he had earned his Doctorate of Laws degree from the University of British Columbia. I would like to thank Dr. Maisie Cardinal and family for permission to include the draft that Harold was working on until he became too ill to work. Dr. Cardinal was a path-breaking and wise leader called upon by many for his experience and expertise; his contributions to Aboriginal politics, law, and understanding between peoples in Canada will continue to have an effect, as will his life's work for the recognition of the spirit and intent of the treaties. The contributors to this volume were deeply saddened by Dr. Cardinal's passing and wanted to write a few words about him as a small way of acknowledging his contributions. These statements appear in "Remembering Harold Cardinal" near the end of this book.

To Doris Wolf and our children, Claire and Simon, thank you for your love and support along this and other journeys.

And finally, my appreciation to the contributors for their hard work, their dedication to this book despite several delays, and for their patience and good humour while working with me, a non-expert in some of the areas addressed: it was a pleasure to work with and learn from you all.

Paul DePasquale
UNIVERSITY OF WINNIPEG
September 30, 2006

NATIVES & SETTLERS · NOW & THEN

Refractions of the Colonial Past in the Present

Paul W. DePasquale

ON APRIL 17, 2000, the Medieval and Early Modern Institute presented the interdisciplinary conference "Natives and Settlers Now and Then" at the University of Alberta, featuring several distinguished scholars in the area of Indigenous Studies: now-deceased Aboriginal political leader, Harold Cardinal, who in 2001 was awarded the Lifetime Achievement Award from the National Aboriginal Achievement Awards for his significant contributions to Aboriginal and treaty rights in Canada; Patricia Seed, professor of history at the University of California, Irvine, and author of several highly acclaimed books; Frank Tough, professor of Native Studies at the Faculty of Native Studies, University of Alberta, and principal investigator of the Métis Archival Project; and Cree lawyer Sharon Venne, recipient of numerous awards and author of influential studies in the area of oral traditions and Indigenous rights.

I was honoured to have been invited to help organize this event. I had recently completed my doctoral studies in English at the University of Alberta, with a focus on representations of Aboriginal peoples in early-modern European colonial writings. As a student of early colonialism and a person of Aboriginal ancestry, I had often been struck by the ways in which the historical past continues to exert pressure on the lives of present-day Aboriginal peoples. It had often seemed to me that the historical, political, and legal issues surrounding North America's colonial past and neocolonial present were not often discussed at the post-secondary level, not in the humanities, even though these issues are of increasing relevance to many of us whose work crosses various disciplines and borders. So the idea of an interdisciplinary event that drew attention to historical and contemporary issues of continuing relevance to Aboriginal peoples struck me as exciting and innovative.

The conference was dynamic, charged with ideas, enjoyed by and of benefit to students and faculty from various departments and to members of the larger community. Addressing such subjects as treaties, treaty-making, Aboriginal rights and title, land claims, identity, representations, education, and nation-building in the Canadian context, the event had an international scope as well, through Sharon Venne's years of experience at the United Nations and Patricia Seed's comparative studies of European colonialism and of treaties in Canada, the United States, and New Zealand.

These presentations and discussions, first recorded and transcribed, and now revised, updated, and printed here for the first time, seem even more relevant today than they did when first delivered. It is clear that, while there have been several developments at the political and legal levels in recent years, the majority of Aboriginal peoples are still unable to access the benefits, rights, and privileges enjoyed by other Canadian citizens. The codes and texts through which racism and xenophobia are perpetuated may have shifted, but there is little evidence that most Native peoples are not still bound by old and familiar patterns of perception. Talk of the "postcolonial" in this country, as in other formerly colonized countries, is academic: on the few occasions when the term "postcolonial" is employed by Indigenous thinkers, it is used either to denounce the terminology of an ill-fitting Western theoretical discourse or to describe a hypothetical route to an imaginary future. As Mi'kmaq educator Marie Battiste writes in *Reclaiming Indigenous Voice and Vision*, the Indigenous scholars in her collection use the term "postcolonial"

> to describe a symbolic strategy for shaping a desirable future, not an existing reality. The term is an aspirational practice, goal, or idea...used to imagine a new form of society that they desired to create. Yet we recognized that postcolonial societies do not exist. Rather, we acknowledged the colonial mentality and structures that still exist in all societies and nations and the neocolonial tendencies that resist decolonization in the contemporary world. (xix)

Battiste's words convey a hopeful skepticism shared by many Aboriginal peoples, who critique the postcolonial on the grounds that its theoretical discourses fail to describe adequately the experience and reality of those who continue to be subject to colonialist processes and strategies here in Canada.

The need today to shape a society that resists colonial mentalities and structures as it encourages the full participation of Aboriginal peoples is foregrounded by increasing disparities between Native and settler peoples. The threat of globalism to indigenous cultures and languages is by now well understood. Less considered in academic contexts are the material realities existing in Canada that signify an abysmal failure on the part of our institutions, particularly our educational systems. Despite the so-called "progress" of contemporary society, the statistics relating to every aspect of Aboriginal peoples' lives and livelihood in Canada today—statistics on education, poverty, housing, crime, employment, and health indicate that the present conditions and future outlook for the majority of Aboriginal peoples are deplorable and grim. In the province where I live, Manitoba, the average life expectancy of Aboriginal people lags behind the general population by eight years for men and seven for women; mortality rates for Aboriginal children aged one to four are four times higher than the Canadian average; suicide rates among youth aged 15–24 are five times the national average for males and seven times for females; the Aboriginal proportion of the prison population is about 70 percent for men, higher for women; Aboriginal peoples are far less likely than the general population to complete high school and attend university and far more likely to contract serious illnesses such as diabetes and heart disease; Aboriginal peoples living on reserve often live in delapidated, overcrowded homes (*Aboriginal People in Manitoba*). According to a recent study by the Institute of Urban Studies, while many Aboriginal peoples move to Winnipeg in search of a better life, nearly 50 percent end up homeless because they are unable to find work and adequate housing (O'Brien). On September 27, 2006, several hundred First Nations people marched to the Manitoba Legislative Building as part of a nationwide protest against cutbacks in federal health and other programs, at a time when the Canadian Cancer Society has reported alarming increases in the number of Manitoba Aboriginal people diagnosed with breast, prostate, lung, and colon cancer.[1]

Such present-day realities have a long trajectory in North America, dating to a time before the federal government's implementation of the Indian Act of 1876 and the colonial strategies engendered by that paternalistic legislation, such as residential schools. As the following essays demonstrate in different ways, the present is heavily informed by the earliest encounters between Aboriginals and Europeans, when Western assumptions about non-European "savages" began to take shape as colonialist ideology. The contradictory tropes of the noble and ignoble Indian first articulated in the writings associated with Columbus's four voyages, reinforced by sixteenth- and seventeenth-century English writings on

America and its peoples, gave rise to the racist stereotypes and assumptions that made post-Enlightenment colonialism possible, even perhaps inevitable. And the assumptions about Good and Bad Indians that evolved during the Renaissance, static ideas about welcoming, friendly Indians on the one hand and ignorant savages on the other, remain with us in numerous contemporary configurations (see Francis).

Marie Battiste states that colonial structures and tendencies "can only be resisted and healed by reliance on Indigenous knowledge and its imaginative processes" (xix). While an increased awareness of Aboriginal epistemologies and perspectives would undoubtedly encourage positive social change, it is also increasingly important for the mainstream population to better understand the European history of colonialism in North America, and the ways European knowledges intersected, often clashed, with Aboriginal knowledges. The mainstream population knows very little–is being very little taught–about the historic relations between Natives and settlers, and why and in what forms these historic relations continue to play out in the present.

The city where I live, Winnipeg, continues to face the challenges of other Canadian cities with a large urban Aboriginal population. While this heterogeneous community has the potential to be an international leader in the area of human rights,[2] the day-to-day relations between its non-Aboriginal and Aboriginal populations (comprised mainly of Anishinaabe, Cree, Métis, Dene, and some Inuit peoples) are often strained. A recent controversy involved city council's release in September 2003 of its 15-point strategy to reduce poverty and improve housing and employment for Aboriginal peoples, called "First Steps: Municipal Urban Aboriginal Pathways." A major part of this strategy is urban reserves, something most members of the public know little about but seem to fear a great deal. The main criticism expressed in all public discourses is that urban reserves will give unfair tax advantages and other incentives to Aboriginal businesses, although the tone of the criticism also suggests that many are anxious about the idea of an Indian reserve being built right in our own backyard. City councillor John Angus observed, "The word 'reserve' causes everyone to have fits." Poplar River's Raven Thundersky pointed out that while Saskatchewan has 21 urban reserves, Winnipegers spring into hostile reaction at the thought of one here (Sanders and "Mayor Will Fight for Urban Reserves"). An editorial in the *Winnipeg Free Press* commented on this "hostile reaction":

> The word "reserve" evokes, in some people's minds, an expanse
> of land where the native people live and where, every now and

then, they set up road blocks to stop traffic on the highway. If you transplant that image into Winnipeg, you get the idea that there's going to be a district of Winnipeg that will be run by a band council, where the city's authority will not run and where people who are not members of the band may not be welcome. ("Reserve Judgment")

Sixty percent of Winnipegers demanded a referendum on the issue while then Mayor Glen Murray drew much criticism by stating that there would be a plebiscite like the one that blocked an urban reserve casino proposal in Thompson, Manitoba, "over my dead body," adding that he wouldn't let "the tyranny of the majority" overrule rights to which First Nations are entitled through treaties signed generations ago ("Mayor Will Fight for Urban Reserves").[3]

The linguists Kress and van Leeuwen argue that Western traditions of representing "otherness" through written discourse may be coming to an end and that visual codes are replacing textual ones in late modernity (Hallam and Street 8).[4] Of course, visual representations of "others" in Western traditions have since ancient times conveyed assumptions both about the centre of humanity and the forms of homomonstrosity imagined to dwell at the centre's edge. Europeans since the earliest contacts in America, and the English since the 1580s, have recognized the ideological value of visual representations of Aboriginal peoples that are unequivocally negative or positive, rarely neutral or what we might think of as realistic (DePasquale, "Re-Writing the Virginian Paradise"). Like the visual codes of the past, today's signifying texts produced by non-Aboriginal peoples include a range of images of romanticized or vilified Indians, commodified in Hollywood movies, sports team logos, and on product labels, or used by media, sometimes only, it seems, to affirm mainstream assumptions. In Winnipeg there are hotels named after Indian nations, located on busy streets with Indian names, using large neon signs with noble savage imagery to promote lodging, ladies' night, and cold beer sales. An article in the newspaper on Winnipegers' hostile reaction to the recent ban on public indoor smoking is illustrated by a photo of a group of Natives smoking outside of a casino in wintertime. To promote hydroelectric development in the North, particularly the $1-billion-dollar Wuskwatim hydroelectric generating project currently under construction in partnership with the Nisichawayasihk Cree Nation, Manitoba Hydro paints a mural on one of its buildings of a young Native female, smiling, arms outstretched in welcoming gesture, a pristine wilderness as background.[5] The caption, "protect *my* environment," reflects a ventriloquism not unlike that deployed by English colonialists of the late sixteenth century who, as a way to promote westward expansion, constructed the image of the welcoming Indian in need of the superior European power's protection and aid. These sorts of everyday representations produced by non-Aboriginals contribute to the misperceptions of a mainstream public that is already uneducated about, but generally disinclined to support, Aboriginal issues.

To counteract the negative public image of urban reserves, the *Winnipeg Free Press* printed information about the Manitoba Treaty Land Entitlement Framework Agreement (MTLEFA), which makes the creation of urban reserves possible. Signed in 1997 between 19 First Nations (which became 20 when one split into two), Canada, and Manitoba, the agreement makes land available to the 20 First Nations in an effort to settle the debt owed because these nations did not receive all land promised under Treaties 1, 2, 3, 4, 5, 6, and 10. 14 signatories to the MTLEFA have begun settling their claims, and six are eligible to build an urban reserve in any city or town in Manitoba. Manitoba is the only Western province without an urban reserve; British Columbia has about 30, Saskatchewan 20, and Alberta one (Sanders; Sinclair). The paper also published details of a public forum organized by city council to reassure Winnipegers that urban reserves would not lead to what many said they feared: a depressed eyesore with derelict cars and house trailers, a place of lawnessness, cigarette smuggling, gun running, or businesses that led to increased taxes or the failure of non-Aboriginal businesses. "I learned a lot," said one retired woman from the affluent neighborhood of Tuxedo. "Some people came here rather afraid, but we'll go home feeling much different. I have a better understanding of the issue" ("Public Forum Eases Urban Reserve Fears"). Once historical facts and actual experiences were made available, the controversy surrounding urban reserves eased up a little and currently awaits the outcome of several proposals by Manitoba bands, not without ongoing public criticism.[6]

The urban reserve controversy suggests that a significant obstacle to the socio-economic health and revitalization of Aboriginal peoples today is not always a lack of political will, for both Winnipeg's former mayor Glen Murray and present mayor Sam Katz have publicly stated their support for urban reserves, but, rather, deeply engrained assumptions held by mainstream peoples. The challenge is one of education: with few exceptions, the non-Aboriginal students I teach have had little or no introduction before university to the kinds of issues that might encourage an understanding of the realities facing Aboriginals. For example, I have often wondered how it is possible that here in Winnipeg, the city with the highest percentage of First Nations and Métis people in Canada and the birthplace of Manitoba's founder Louis Riel, so few students are taught anything before university about the Manitoba Métis Federation's quarter-century-old land claim, currently in the courts, to about 1.4 million acres of land in and around Winnipeg, a claim amounting to several billions of dollars. That mainstream peoples routinely inhabit and travel on lands once belonging to Aboriginal peoples, travel on streets with Aboriginal names, without considering the historical processes that made the land available for settler peoples, suggests the ongoing failure of our educational systems.[7] Students seem to hear even less about national issues, unless, of course, media reports some crisis that only confirms stereotypes of Aboriginal peoples as easily agitated and prone to violence, such as the recent Six Nations blockade of disputed lands in Caledonia, Ontario.

Similar attitudes are reflected in a broader North American context that tolerates and even supports ignorance on the subject of Aboriginal issues. While most recognize that overt forms of racist thought are no longer acceptable, many support implicit forms, such as the continuing appropriation of Aboriginal images and voices by a wide range of non-Aboriginal industries—Hollywood movies, automobiles, oil and gas, tobacco, sports, food and health, and even flooring materials. Such industries profit from the production of images that are often historically and culturally inaccurate and sometimes demeaning of the peoples represented. Mainstream North America largely ignores or elides Aboriginal perspectives and actively disavows its colonial legacy. For example, a tourist could take the guided walking tour of Historic Jamestowne in Virginia, the site commemorating the first permanent English settlement in America founded in 1607, jointly administered by the Association for the Preservation of Virginia Antiquities and the National Park Service, and not hear anything unless he asks about the powerful Powhatan Algonquian peoples who occupied and controlled much of the eastern seaboard at the time of English arrival, or their near-genocide by settler peoples.[8] I was surprised on a recent tour when our guide stopped at the rather imposing statue of Captain John Smith, gazed up admiringly, then announced that Smith was his favourite of all English explorers. Our guide spoke enthusiastically of the lively and youthful Pocahontas, who at around thirteen years of age performed cartwheels in the nude right around this very spot to entertain her English guests. He offered, "To the ladies present, I invite you to perform a few cartwheels of your own if you would like to re-enact that early moment in our great nation's history." Our tour ended at William Ordway Partridge's statue of Pocahontas, arms outstretched in her famously welcoming, calmly submissive gesture.[9] We were then invited to have a look around the gift shop, where visitors are greeted by rows of smiling Indian dolls, hair in braids, wearing beaded head-bands and buckskin dresses, with names like "Smiling Beauty" and "Baby Indian Princess." If, as Stuart Hall believes, communication is always linked to power and meaning is in part evoked by what is not said (see *Representations*), then it is easy to understand the need to disavow the history of colonialism and make Aboriginal peoples complicit in and even somehow forgiving of their fate. Among the results of this disavowal in the United States today is a lack of constitutional protection for the legal rights of American Indians and their treaties so that current definitions of Indian rights and sovereignty are largely inconsequential (see Deloria and Wilkins).

Here at home, because young people are taught little about Canada's colonial history, even many intelligent, well-intentioned undergraduates bristle when informed that the federal government spends over $8 billion every year on programs such as education, health, social assistance, and housing. The majority arrive at university steeped in all the negative assumptions and stereotypes, believing on some fundamental level that Aboriginal peoples themselves are responsible for the high rates of unemployment, poverty, incarceration, and poor health in their communities. It is often a challenge to encourage students to engage in a process of "decolonizing the mind," a process that for Métis scholar Melissa Nelson includes "questioning my certainty about things [and asking,] where do my thoughts and ideas come from?" (116). The things that young non-Aboriginal peoples often regard as "handouts" to Aboriginal peoples—education, medical care, and social assistance—are, from the perspective of many, rights promised under the terms of the historic treaties.

Resistance to change is strongest when people believe that they or their communities will be negatively affected in some way. A good example is the recent controversy that attracted national attention surrounding the name of Morden Collegiate's hockey team, the Morden Mohawks, now renamed Morden Thunder. In 2002, then grade twelve student Meghan Menzies initiated the debate in this small Mennonite farming community in Manitoba after considering that the forty-year-old name and team crest with an image of a screaming Mohawk warrior might be offensive to some. The majority of students and community residents, approximately 86 per cent according to a recent ballot, believe that the name change is an insult to former graduates. "Mohawks are who we are and who we've been," protested one student. Another agreed, "I think our name should stay—our parents graduated as Mohawks." Some feel that the name honours Aboriginal peoples and traditions. "These people should lighten up," one local resident stated. "[The name] denotes a certain kind of person—there's fear, aggression, respect. You're a hockey team, come on. If I made a hockey team called Mohawks, I'd say 'hey, I've done something.'" Others disagree. Terry Nelson, chief of nearby Roseau River First Nation, questioned, "If I put a team together in Roseau River, how about the Ojibway Mennonites? How about the Morden Jews? The Morden French? If my Ojibway Mennonites team scores a goal and I go [drawing a cross in the air with his hand], do you find that offensive, or am I honouring you?" ("Morden School to Drop Mohawks Name").[10]

If the collective will to uphold traditions that engendered the appropriation of Aboriginal imagery for use in sports remains entrenched, the controversy surrounding urban reserves in Winnipeg suggests that settler peoples will vigorously contest Aboriginal entitlement to lands based upon assumptions rooted in the past. A letter to the editor of the *Winnipeg Free Press*, published on October 24, 2003 in the context of public debates about the meaning of the historic treaties, illustrates this tendency:

> When I read the treaties covering the area from eastern Ontario
> to the Rocky Mountains, I see the words "(the Indians) do hereby
> cede, release, surrender, and yield up to Her Majesty the Queen...
> all the lands..." in Treaties 1 and 2, and the words "(the Indians)
> doe hereby cede, release, surrender, and yield up...all their rights,
> titles and privileges whatsoever to the land..." in Treaties 3 to 7.
> I cannot understand how anyone can claim that the treaties are
> simply an agreement for peaceful coexistence with an extremely
> limited transfer of land rights.... Wishful thinking cannot change
> fact. (Uchtmann)

Government representatives and settler societies have employed this same narrow thinking for years in order to justify the expropriation of Aboriginal lands. As Jean Friesen explains, "To the [treaty] commissioners as to most Canadians then and now, the treaties were considered a 'once and for all' way of clearing the land of the legal obligations of Indian title" (210).[11]

Several interconnected colonial myths inform the view that Indians gave up their lands at the time of treaty-making. One is the myth of the passive, unsophisticated Indian who easily submits to superior European technologies. This myth entered Western consciousness through Columbus's perceptions of the "simple" and naked inhabitants of the Caribbean, the Taino and Arawaks, who believed, according to Europeans, that the travellers had come from the heavens. The myth of the passive and simple Indian has affected the expectations of travellers, writers, colonizers, and artists ever since, even though the documentary evidence shows that Aboriginal peoples from the earliest efforts to colonize North America possessed an experience and agency in areas like warfare and trade that seriously undermine claims of European mastery in the new world (DePasquale, "'Worth the Noting'"). This history is consistent with evidence that suggests that nineteenth-century Indian politicians and diplomats exercised a great deal of agency when they negotiated the historic treaties (Friesen 206).

Another colonial myth is rooted in unquestioned assumptions about the perceived right and legal authority of Christians to occupy foreign territories (Washburn, *Red Man's Land*). English justifications for the expropriation of foreign lands were first expressed in Thomas More's *Utopia* (1516), the earliest English attempt to elaborate a theory of colonization (Quinn). More wrote that land could legitimately be taken "[w]hen any people holdeth a piece of ground void and vacant to no good or profitable use: keeping others from the use and possession of it, which, notwithstanding, by the law of nature, ought therefore to be nourished and relived" (book 2, chapter 5). According to Wilcomb Washburn, colonizers employed three main arguments to expropriate Indian lands, each justified by the Old Testament: God made room for settlers through gift, purchase, or legitimate expulsion of heathens by war. A foreign people could also occupy vacant lands without permission or purchase in order to cultivate them ("The Moral and Legal Justification"). The European assumption of easy and lawful access to lands in America, reinforced by missionary rhetoric, provided the foundation for post-Enlightenment colonialism in North America, engendering processes, such as treaty-making under John A. Macdonald's Conservative government in the late nineteenth century, intended to transfer vast areas of interest and control of lands from Aboriginal peoples to settlers (see Stonechild and Waiser).

The above letter also reflects a lack of awareness of contemporary developments in Canadian politics and law concerning the "spirit" of the treaties, as distinct from their written form. In the 1973 "Statement on Claims of Indian and Inuit People," one of the early federal statements on treaty policy in modern times, then Minister of Indian and Northern Affairs Jean Chrétien announced that the Canadian government "recognizes the importance of full compliance with the spirit and term of your treaties" (qtd. in Price xiii). Important as an anticipation of future directions, this statement had little effect on the courts because, as Price explains, the Crown tends to limit interpretations of the historic treaties to the strict written terms and is strongly influenced by the Euro-Canadian court system, although the courts have become more open to trying to understand both Aboriginal and government perspectives (Price xiii). In 1996, the Royal Commission Report on Aboriginal Peoples recommended that "[j]ustice requires the fulfillment of the agreed terms of the treaties, as recorded in the treaty text and supplemented by oral evidence" (2.2.2, qtd. in Price ix). The 1997 Supreme Court of Canada Delgamuukw decision further supported oral histories by deeming that they need to be taken into account along with other evidence.

In recent years scholars have acknowledged the importance of reciprocity behind the historic treaties and agreements made between the Crown and First Nations across Canada, between, that is, nations considered sovereign at the time of treaty-making, according to interpretations of Section 35 of the Constitution Act of 1982. Part 1 of this section "recognizes and affirms" the "existing aboriginal and treaty rights of the aboriginal peoples of Canada."[12] The Royal Proclamation of 1763, the first pre-confederation treaty, began the European process of treaty-making in Canada by acknowledging the need for the consent of First Nations in negotiations for their land. Recognizing the role of First Nations as allies in Great Britain's military struggle against France, the Royal Proclamation promised not to allow agricultural settlement of Indian territories until Aboriginal peoples first ceded land to the Crown through treaties. The policy of negotiating for Crown control of Indian lands continued through the late eighteenth and nineteenth centuries with other pre-confederation treaties, such as the Selkirk Treaty of 1817, signed by Saulteaux and Cree First Nations and the Government of Canada; the Robinson Treaty of 1850, signed by Anishinaabe First Nations and the Government of Canada; and the Manitoulin Island Treaty of 1862, signed by Ottawa, Chippewa, and other First Nations and the Government of Canada. Treaty-making was well established around 1868 when the Hudson's Bay Company ceded Ruperts Land and North Western Territory to the Crown (Stonechild and Waiser 6–7).

Following Confederation, eleven numbered treaties between First Nations stretching from James Bay to the Rockies and the Government of Canada were negotiated between 1871 and 1929. In the government view, Aboriginal peoples agreed upon land surrender and the maintenance of peace in exchange for benefits that varied from treaty to treaty but generally included a small cash annuity, reserves of land, schools, agricultural assistance, and hunting and fishing supplies (Taylor 3–7).[13] More recent comprehensive claims agreements involving land and self-government have been settled since 1973, when the federal government, following the Supreme Court of Canada's Calder decision, first recognized Aboriginal land rights based on Aboriginal title. These agreements include the James

Bay and Northern Quebec Agreement (1975), the Northeastern Quebec Agreement (1978), the Gwich'in Agreement (1992), the Nunavut Land Claims Agreement (1993), the Sahtu Dene and Métis Agreement (1994), and the Nisga'a Final Agreement (2000).

For much of the twentieth century the historic treaties have been interpreted by scholars not as the sacred commitments they are to many Aboriginal peoples, but as tragic examples, writes Jean Friesen, "of 'misunderstanding' or of the ignorance of Indian leaders" (204). This so-called "ignorance," one of the colonial myths I examined above, was recently put into perspective for me by Omushkego ("Swampy Cree") historian Louis Bird, of Winisk First Nation. Bird discussed David Sutherland (ca. 1880–1963), the brother of his grandmother, Maggie Sutherland, and one of three signatories of the Treaty Nine adhesion around 1930, an extension of the 1905 treaty. In 1957, David Sutherland was interviewed by missionaries about his experiences, including the treaty-making. The original reel-to-reel tapes in Cree were destroyed sometime after the Winisk flood in 1986, but an English translation of the interview is part of Bird's oral history collection.[14] Louis Bird explained that some of Sutherland's responses when the priests asked him about the treaty were not recorded and are therefore not part of the historical record. According to Bird, David Sutherland was frustrated and disappointed on the subject of the treaty:

David said,

"I don't understand the treaty. I don't know the meaning of this treaty. He [the commissioner] talks about the land, but that's not the way I see the land. I didn't think anyone possessed the land." [The commissioner] talked about the way he uses the land, and the idea didn't make any sense to David. He just didn't understand. Too much, too far different idea. So he just listened, didn't ask another question. There were three of them, my grandfather too, and also Xavier Patrick. And the three Elders were sitting there, but they didn't understand exactly what the treaty-making mean. And the land? To give the land—your land—in exchange for what? And then the priest asked David, "Didn't you ask any questions at all to these commissioners?" And he says, "No. No way." After negotiating, they were sent home to go to bed and talk to the people. Which they didn't. They talked about it a little bit amongst themselves. It was too late, and they were so confused, according to them. So finally, "Well, we might as well just sign the papers." And that's how they submit. And the next morning, the commissioner says, "Okay. You have been informed about the treaty, and the treaty represented the three of you, the three Elders have signed the agreement. Now that's done. Now we have to elect a chief." So they elected a chief. Xavier was elected chief because he was younger. And then after they elected a chief—which they did very quickly—the commissioner says, "Okay. You are the chief. We give you this badge, and this flag, to represent that you submit to this magistrate's government which will protect you, and you abide by the law, and you will be subject." The translator was not saying exactly what the commissioner said. The translator said: "The law will be given and the government will protect you." That's how this treaty was. And then Xavier was asked, "Do you have any questions?" The chief was supposed to speak and question things. He didn't. He was a leader amongst the people. So he was supposed to speak at that time when they were sitting with the commissioners. He was supposed to ask questions, but he didn't. Xavier just submitted, that's what David said. He just said, "Yes, yes, okay," and that's all he said. He didn't ask questions. And after that it was too late to ask because they'd already signed the treaty. David was saying that, in offense [upset, disappointed], when he was talking to the priest. And he says, "Unfortunately, we did not comprehend what was happening."[15]

The treaty relations and negotiations between Natives and settlers from the nineteenth to the early twentieth centuries were unequal, guided by two very different sets of principles regarding land ownership. While traditional Aboriginal relationships with the land were communal and conservationist (Usher), Euro-Canadians were motivated primarily by private and commercial interests. From the perspective of many who have traditionally viewed Aboriginal peoples as stewards of the land for the Creator, it is inconceivable that those at the time of the treaty could possibly have agreed to "cede, release and surrender and yield up to the Government of the Dominion...all their rights, titles and privileges..." as is written in the treaty texts (Price xiv).[16] The knowledge and values of Aboriginal peoples that shaped principles antithetical to European objectives should certainly not be misinterpreted as an indication of ignorance.[17]

With numerous outstanding grievances in Canada today, including a backlog of over 1,000 unsettled land claims cases affecting much of Canada and most of British Columbia, we are at a critical period in Native and settler relations today. Expectations—and doubts in this post-Kelowna

Accord era—are high today for the resolution of outstanding grievances. Aboriginal peoples first took collective action in an effort to redress treaty issues when Chief Beardy of the Willow Cree hosted a council in the summer of 1884 (Stonechild and Waiser 60). In June 1970, Harold Cardinal suggested to Prime Minister Pierre Trudeau that Indian claims be handed over to an impartial claims commission for settlement. Many years later it remains to be seen if effective change can be implemented at the political and legal levels. The ongoing confrontations between residents of Caledonia, Ontario, and members of the Six Nations highlight the mistrust that still exists between Native and settler peoples today, the volatile nature of that mistrust, the failure of governmental policies past and present, and the urgent need for resolution ("This Land is My Land"). Given the uneven distribution of resources and opportunities existing in the nation-state, and increasing tensions on all sides, it requires no stretch of the imagination to say that the safety, well-being, and livelihood of many Canadians are at stake today.[18]

Along with effective resolution, what is needed is an informed, educated citizenry aware of the ways in which past colonialist tendencies and practices continue to shape the realities of Aboriginal peoples. A sustained willingness to engage in education of this kind will help make developments at the political and legal levels meaningful to the majority of Aboriginal peoples, whose access to rights and benefits is often denied not simply by colonialist governments and structures, but by persistent modes of thinking in the broader society.

The following essays and discussions will not resolve any of these tensions, but it is hoped that they will contribute to ongoing debates and raise awareness of the historical and contemporary issues affecting present-day Native and settler peoples.

Natives and Settlers Now and Then: The Essays

In *Indigenous Difference and the Constitution of Canada*, Patrick Macklem argues that Aboriginal participation in treaty-making, along with their status as distinct cultures that occupied and exercised sovereign power over specific territories prior to contact, constitute what he calls "Indigenous difference." Sharon Venne's essay, "Treaties Made in Good Faith," shows that Aboriginal peoples did not merely participate in the treaty-making process; they had developed it long before contact with Europeans as a way to co-exist with neighbouring nations. Venne discusses the meaning and terms of treaty-making in the context of Treaty Six as she has learned it from her Cree Elders. The words the Elders often repeat, "as long as the waters flow," refer, Venne explains, to the Plains Cree belief that the treaty their ancestors negotiated in 1876 at Fort Carlton and Fort Pitt, Saskatchewan, would last for as long as water flows when women give birth. She contextualizes her Plains Cree understanding of Treaty Six by referring to the two agreements Cree peoples reached long ago in present-day Alberta with Blackfoot and Dene peoples. The demarcations imposed by these "living spirits," the peace treaties, continue to be acknowledged by many Aboriginal peoples today. Drawing on her extensive participation with the Working Group on Indigenous Peoples at the United Nations, Venne then offers a promising examination of how international mechanisms are contributing to a better understanding of the importance of Canada's historic treaties.

The colonizer's preoccupation with land is nothing new, as Patricia Seed shows in "Three Treaty Nations Compared: Economic and Political Consequences for Indigenous Peoples in Canada, the United States, and New Zealand." England has in fact been preoccupied with land ownership since the Middle Ages. She traces the foundation of the English legal system to ownership of soil and finds that the first official legal acts of English sovereignty in the New World, Queen Elizabeth's letters patent in the late sixteenth century, established this pattern by entitling Sir Humphrey Gilbert and Walter Ralegh to "have, hold, occupy, and enjoy all the soil" in the newly discovered territories. Land ownership constituted the cultural heart of the English invention of America as theirs. Since occupation of the soil and distributing it according to English law were the officially designated goals of English colonization, it is not surprising that the central concern of Aboriginal peoples subject to an English colonial system is to restore land and resource ownership in the present day.

The preoccupation with land ownership led to the development in the late nineteenth and early twentieth centuries of processes, such as the numbered treaties, intended to extinguish Aboriginal title. Often overlooked are similar strategies the Crown implemented in order to extinguish Métis Aboriginal title. In "'The Rights to the Land May Be Transferred': Archival Records as Colonial Text—A Narrative of Métis Scrip," Frank Tough and Erin McGregor provide the first in-depth examination of the Métis of Northwest Saskatchewan's land claim against the governments of Canada and Saskatchewan. By reconstructing the paper trail relating to Eli Roy, a Métis man who in 1906 was granted, but never received, 240 acres of land, Tough and McGregor expose the realities and inequities of the colonial scrip system that prevented many Saskatchewan Métis from taking ownership of lands to which they were entitled.

Discussing the "predatory mentality of Eurocentric thought" in Western academic disciplines, Marie Battiste and James (Sa'ke'j) Youngblood

Henderson in *Protecting Indigenous Knowledge and Heritage: A Global Challenge* (2000) deconstruct this cognitive imperialism in an effort to negotiate a path for Indigenous heritages and perspectives. John Borrows, in *Recovering Canada: The Resurgence of Indigenous Law* (2002), uses examples from Ojibwe oral traditions and the Six Nations Two-Row Wampum to indicate ways in which First Nations and Canada can integrate competing worldviews into a renewed vision of Canada's constitution. In his essay "Nation-Building: Reflections of a Nihiyow [Cree]," Harold Cardinal reflects on his many years of experience as a political leader and scholar of both Western and traditional Cree knowledges. The process of decolonization and nation-building is fairly new in Canada, slowly underway since the patriation of the British North America Act in 1982. Aboriginal peoples today must examine several important questions. Because of the negative effect on communities and families of legal definitions of "Indians" under the Indian Act, including Bill C-31, the most urgent question, according to Elders, is *Awina maga kee anow,* or "Who is it that we really are?" Cardinal discusses the lessons to be learned from a comparative analysis of Western and Aboriginal knowledges, and shows how Elders can be involved in the process. Examining the most comprehensive doctrine of law among Cree peoples, known as *Wa-koo-to-win,* the law governing human relationships, Cardinal explains the continuing vitality of this doctrine in an era of treaty implementation and a newer understanding between nations.

About the Editorial Process

Harold Cardinal and Frank Tough's original presentations were delivered with the use of only a few notes, and, in Tough's case, overheads. Sharon Venne used no notes during her presentation, preferring, she explained to me afterward, to speak without notes as a way of exercising the abilities the Creator gave her. Patricia Seed spoke informally and read from parts of her book *American Pentimento: The Pursuit of Riches and the Invention of "Indians."* The audiocassette recordings of the original presentations, questions, and discussions were transcribed by Nancy Van Styvendale. These transcribed talks were then sent to the contributors with a request for correction and revision. Frank Tough enlisted the assistance of Erin McGregor to help develop his presentation into essay form. The individual essays went back and forth between me and the contributors many times, with comments and suggestions intended to improve the flow and understanding of material for readers, including students and non-experts. Contributors were invited to maintain the informal diction and other oral qualities of their original presentations, since all involved agreed from the beginning that the finished book would do well to reflect the sense of dialogue and ongoing discussion that made the original event so rewarding and memorable.

The terminology Aboriginal peoples use to describe themselves and their communities varies widely and has not been standardized. I have left such decisions, including decisions about which words to capitalize, up to the contributors. Also, I have not imposed guidelines that might have resulted in greater consistency between the essays; because of their unique subject matter and the expertise and interests of individual contributors, they vary in both form and content. Despite their many differences, the essays gathered here tell a coherent and mostly lamentable story about the interactions between Native and settler peoples in historical and contemporary times.

NOTES

1 On the "disgrace of the third-world conditions" in Aboriginal education, employment, and health in Manitoba, see "Aboriginal Schooling." See also Michael Lawrenchuk's documentary on the living conditions in northern Manitoba, *As Long as the Sun Shines*. See also Aboriginal Task Group, Rabson, and Skerritt.

2 Still in the works despite government cutbacks to museums across the nation are plans to build the Canadian Museum for Human Rights, projected to open in Winnipeg in 2010 at a cost of over $300 million (www.canadianmuseumforhumanrights.com). The museum is expected to educate over 100,000 visitors each year about historical human rights abuses in Canada and around the world. The museum has been called "Canada's gift to the world, a means of highlighting this country's dedication to the belief that human rights are inalienable, the cornerstone of peaceful and civilized society" ("A Liberal Contribution").

3 On the criticism against Murray, see "Mayor Defends Reserves" and the letters to the editor devoted to the controversy in the *Winnipeg Free Press*. 13 Sept. 2003: A17. Glen Murray defended his position in "Treaty is a Treaty, Deal is a Deal."

4 Stuart Hall regards visual media as the privileged sign of late modern culture. See Hall, "Representation and the Media"; and Hall, *Representations: Cultural Representations and Signifying Practices*.

5 Construction of the controversial generating station on the Burntwood River in northern Manitoba began on August 11, 2006, after much debate and division among members of northern communities still affected by Manitoba Hydro flooding at Cross Lake over 25 years ago. The mural can be viewed at http://www.manitobawildlands.org/develop_hydro.htm.

6 See, for example, Herb Schulz's letter to the editor of October 2, 2006, "Urban Reserves a Tax Dodge." For details about the history of urban reserves and highly successful models in Saskatchewan, see F. Laurie Barron and Joseph Garcea, eds., *Urban Reserves: Forging New Relationships in Saskatchewan*.

7 In a 2002 telephone survey of over twenty non-Aboriginal businesses and institutions listed

in the Winnipeg white pages with the word "Dakota" in their name, several located on
busy Dakota Street along the Assiniboine River, not one representative could say why the
word "Dakota" was in their business's name, or anything beyond the simple association of
"Dakota" with "a tribe of Indians." Taking a guess at why the word "Dakota" appears in his
own school's name, one senior administrator offered, "We're located on Dakota Street—I'm
assuming that's how it works."

Allies with the British beginning with the Treaty of Paris in 1763 and loyal throughout the
American Revolution in 1776 and in the war against Britain in 1812, Dakota peoples were
stripped of their vast lands through several treaties with the Americans from 1815 to 1851.
Seeking refuge from American persecution south of the border, the first bands of Dakota
reached the Red River settlement in the early 1860s, inhabited parts of the city along the
Assiniboine River, and eventually re-settled on several Dakota reservations throughout
Manitoba as the city of Winnipeg grew (Elias 9–19).

8 On the precontact history of Powhatan peoples, see Helen C. Rountree, *Pocahontas's People*
and *The Powhatan Indians of Virginia*.

9 An online tour of Historic Jamestowne is available at http://www.apva.org/tour/pocastat.
html. Not surprisingly, at this website celebrating the English settlement there is an
absence of information about the significance of Powhatan Algonquian peoples and their
near genocide, though readers will find links to details about the frequently romanticized
life of Pocahontas and numerous references to ambushes, attacks, and killings by Indians
(see http://historicjamestowne.org/index.php). Gearing up for the 400th anniversary of
Jamestown, much is made, however, of the discovery since 1994 of over 1 million objects
relating to the English colonists and their way of life at James Fort. The most celebrated
discovery to date is the remains of a high-ranking colonist, possibly Captain Bartholomew
Gosnold, the principal organizer and administrator of the early Jamestown effort.

The Pocahontas statue was planned in 1906 to mark the 300th Jamestown anniversary
but not unveiled until 1922, due to the difficulty of securing funding for the project in an
era when, according to William Rasmussen and Robert Tilton, "Pocahontas had two strikes
against her: she was an Indian and an independent woman" (44). For details on the statue's
"dramatic, theatrical stance" and "visually appealing" but culturally inaccurate dress and
design, see Rasmussen and Tilton 43–44. Their book, *Pocahontas: Her Life & Legend* (1994),
published by the Virginia Historical Society with support from The Walt Disney Company,
concludes with a glowing assessment of Disney's animated film, *Pocahontas* (1994).

10 See also "Board Tells School to Pick Team Name" and "Morden's Mohawks are History."

11 The following three paragraphs are a development of my response to this letter, "Recognize
Spirit of Treaties."

12 For debates surrounding the issue of Aboriginal self-government arising out of Section 35 of
the Constitution Act, 1982, see the bibliography at
http://www.ainc-inac.gc.ca/pr/trts/hti/bib/con_e.html.

13 The texts of the Selkirk Treaty, the Robinson Treaty, the Manitoulin Island Treaty, and treaties
one through seven are available in Morris. For useful timelines, maps, and full text versions
of many historic treaties, see http://www.ainc-inac.gc.ca/pr/trts/hti/site/maindex_e.html.
Aboriginal and treaty rights and the issue of compensation are examined in Mainville.

14 John Long discusses treaty-making at Winisk and the 1957 interview with Sutherland in "Who
Got What at Winisk, Treaty-Making, 1930."

15 Interview with the author. Bird reflects on the effect of the treaty on his people in chapter 9 of
Louis Bird, *Telling Our Stories: Omushkego Legends and Histories from Hudson Bay*.

16 The Ontario District Court in R. v. Battisse (1978) held that in the case of Treaty Nine itself
"the parties to the Agreement were on grossly unequal footings. Highly skilled negotiators

were dealing with illiterate people, who, though fearful of losing their way of life, placed great faith in the fairness of His Majesty, as represented by federal authorities" (qtd. in Imai 31). For a history not unlike that related by Louis Bird, see the details of the Sayisi Dene's signing of the Treaty Five adhesion in 1910, which made land in northern Manitoba available for the northern extension of the railroad from The Pas to Churchill, in Tough "As Resources Fail" 99–113 and Bussidor and Bilgen-Reinart 25–28.

17 Not all treaty negotiations were as one-sided, of course. Eyewitness accounts of the words, actions, and counterdemands of Cree leaders such as Mistawasis, Poundmaker, The Badger, and Ahtahkakoop during Treaty Six negotiations suggest that these leaders were highly aware of the issues and often forthright with their perspectives and concerns (Stonechild and Waiser 5–26).

18 I am also aware that the successful implementation of agreements already reached, such as the Nisga'a and Nunavut Agreements, is another matter entirely. See the keynote addresses and other texts from the "Achieving Objectives" conference, June 27–30, 2006, hosted by the Land Claims Agreement Coalition, available at http://www.consilium.ca/alcc2006/main.html. For a disturbing picture of the obstacles impeding the implementation of "just" Article 23 of the Nunavut Land Claims Agreement, "to increase Inuit participation in government employment in the Nunavut Settlement Area to a representative level," see Thomas Berger's keynote address, 8–14.

ONE

TREATIES MADE IN GOOD FAITH

Sharon H. Venne

Introduction

THIS PRESENTATION IS ABOUT the oral understanding of Treaty Six and the treaty-making in 1876 at Fort Carlton and Fort Pitt, located in present-day Saskatchewan. There are no written notes for this talk, only my memory of those words spoken by the Elders and Chiefs to express the rich and vibrant life of our Peoples. I remember the Elders stating that the Treaty will last "as long as the sun shines, the waters flow, and the grass grows."[1] The words "the waters flow" refer, not to a body of water like the North Saskatchewan River, but to the water that breaks when a woman gives birth. Because the Treaty is supposed to last for as long as water flows when women give birth, these words tie Cree women like me to the Treaty process. How that expression came about is an interesting story, but here I want to talk about the oral understanding of treaty-making as I have learned it from my Elders.

Treaty-Making

First, it is important to acknowledge that the University of Alberta is situated on land ancestral to the Papaschase Cree Peoples. I cannot say that it belonged to the Cree because, actually, all the land belongs to the Creation.[2] Under Treaty Six, Cree Peoples agreed to share some of their lands with the Queen's subjects, but certain lands were not to be shared, called "reserved lands." In an abuse of history as well as of the Cree Peoples, the settlers called the areas of land that would not be shared "reserves" and wrote that "Indians" were placed on "reserves."[3] That is a lie. After the treaty-making in 1876 at Fort Pitt, in Cree territory, Chief Papaschase selected the lands that would not be shared for his Peoples and for the future generations.[4] Those reserved lands were to the south, across the North Saskatchewan River from Fort Edmonton that was occupied by the settlers.

Some twelve years later, in 1888, the settlers decided that they did not like having a reserve so close to them. On 19 November 1888, the land was listed for sale.[5] They had an added economic reason: the railway wanted to come up from the south and Papaschase's Peoples were in the way. The government of Canada rigged it up to keep the settlers happy: when Papaschase's Peoples were away hunting in the North, the Indian Agent arranged for the land to be surrendered without a vote. When Papaschase returned, his reserve was gone.[6]

Today the University of Alberta sits on Papaschase's land. There are stories circulating, based on an Indian Affairs survey, that the reserve was east of the present university site, but at the time of treaty-making the chiefs and Elders selected lands based on landmarks and waterways rather than Indian Affairs surveys. Over at the university's faculty club, there is a room dedicated to Chief Papaschase that gives some acknowledgment of his role in this area. So when you're walking around the University of Alberta, you are walking on his land, on Indigenous land.

Actually, all of North America is Indigenous land. At the time of the treaty-making, Indigenous Peoples never gave up the land. When Indigenous Peoples talk about the land and the making of Treaty,[7] we are talking about our life and the life of the future generations. Land is central to the process. We have a relationship with our Creation based on a legal system designed to protect and honour the land. These are the laws that guided Cree Peoples when the Chiefs negotiated and concluded Treaty Six in 1876.

Over the years, I have heard many people say that non-indigenous people brought treaty-making to Indigenous Peoples. This is totally false. It is not true because Indigenous Peoples living on Great Turtle Island have always had treaty-making. You only have to go back a short way in the history of our Cree Peoples, who made treaties with our neighbouring Indigenous nations. There were wars between the nations so there was a need for peace treaties. Peace treaties are known to the Cree. The Cree made a peace treaty with the Dene that is still in place. The Cree-Dene Treaty—concluded before the coming of the non-indigenous peoples—was to demarcate our territories. The demarcation is known as Peace River: north of the Peace River is Dene land, and south of it is Cree territory. When I cross the Peace River going north into Dene territory, I always give thanks to the Dene for letting me come into their territory. I say a prayer to the Cree and Dene Elders who said that we could travel in peace. This is the meaning of a peace treaty. It needs to be lived. It is not an empty phrase or value; it is a living spirit.

When the Cree travel south, the dividing line between the Cree and the Blackfoot Confederacy is a treaty demarcation. Our ancestors said: "From this day forward, we will live in peace with their people; we will not interfere in the Blackfoot territory." It is not for this generation to break the words of the Elders, who made their commitment using their pipes and the prayers before the Creation.

Not many Indigenous or non-indigenous people know about these treaty demarcations because the government of Canada put a map on top of the land and called it "Alberta." Mapping and renaming the lands as an artificial entity created a big mess. However, Indigenous Peoples must not be deterred by these changes but must continue to remember the land and the stories of the land and waters. As Indigenous Peoples, we must remember the treaties and demarcations because we have treaty relations with neighbouring Peoples. The treaties made among Indigenous nations do not cause problems. The treaties made with the settlers are the troublesome ones.

When the Crown's people came to Cree territory to make the treaty, Indigenous Peoples' treaty-making process was well established.[8] It is important to remember that the Crown came to Indigenous Peoples. The Cree did not go to England to make treaty. The Cree Peoples did not go to Ottawa. The Crown sent its representatives to our lands. There was no conquest in Cree territory. There was no war with non-indigenous people. Our territories were not *terra nullius* ("land of no one"), because we were here. As Nations, we had our own governments, our own laws, our own political and legal systems operating in our territories. These were all in place at the time of contact with the colonizers. Our creation stories tell us that there was no *terra nullius*. The Peoples of Great Turtle Island were not living here waiting to be discovered or colonized.

Garden of Eden or Bering Strait?

The Bering Strait theory does not explain the Indigenous Peoples. Cree Peoples did not come across the Bering Strait. It is a strong belief of mine that Great Turtle Island, and the rest of the lands of our Indigenous brothers and sisters to the south of us, was the Garden of Eden, if you follow the Christian Bible and its theories. Our Great Turtle Island is the Garden of Eden. Those tracks going across the Bering Strait are the people expelled from Great Turtle Island. This theory explains the destruction of Great Turtle Island since the settlers arrived from across the Atlantic Ocean. The settlers returned to the Garden of Eden to try to destroy it since they had been expelled. Now it is payback time for Indigenous Peoples, the territories, waters, animals, birds, and everything on Great Turtle Island. This is my view of history. I want someone to show me the evidence to contradict my theory. If Indigenous Peoples crossed the Bering Strait, why did we not bring wheeled vehicles? Were our ancestors that impractical to carry everything across the Bering Strait and leave wheeled vehicles on the other side of the strait?

International Law

Indigenous Peoples were not discovered. There was no *terra nullius*. There were no wars or conquests. These are some of the justifications in international law that would allow non-indigenous peoples to claim our lands and resources. But there is no justification in international law to allow the expropriation of Indigenous lands without our consent. There is only one legal avenue: a treaty must be made with the Indigenous Peoples.[9]

The International Court of Justice decision in the *Western Sahara* case stated that land occupied by a group of people who organized themselves socially and politically could not be considered *terra nullius*.[10] The Court pronounced that the only way for a foreign sovereign to acquire any right to enter into territories that are not *terra nullius* is with the freely informed consent of the original inhabitants through an agreement. This is international law. It has been encoded into British law since the Royal Proclamation of 1763 and Canadian law since the colony was founded.

The colonizers came to the east of Great Turtle Island and gradually moved west. By the middle of the nineteenth century, treaty-making was a necessity.[11] The English monarch sent a Treaty Commissioner, Alexander Morris, to make treaties on behalf of the Crown; he and later Commissioners made similar treaties with the Cree, Saulteaux, Dene, and Assiniboine Peoples. There were no wars and no conquest. The treaty requested by the Crown was for peace and friendship for settlers. The Treaty Commissioner came with these words, "Let our people live in peace. Let us conclude a peace and friendship Treaty."[12] The Crown knew that the Indigenous Peoples would give nothing else. The Cree leaders told the Commissioner that they would not sell their lands. Besides, Indigenous Peoples outnumbered the non-indigenous; only a few non-indigenous people were scattered throughout our territories, and they did not have the military might to conquer us or even go to war against us. The Commissioner came west and held out his hand in 1876. The treaty the Cree made in 1876 with the non-indigenous people was a peace and friendship treaty. Now, what does that treaty mean?

Commissioner Morris said to our Peoples, "We don't want your animals because we are bringing our own. We don't want your birds because we're bringing our own. And we don't want your fish because we're bringing our own. Everything remains yours. We don't want any of that. We don't have enough money to buy your land." These are some of the words passed down by the Elders about the statements made by the Treaty Commissioner at the treaty-making in 1876. Despite these words, the Crown uses all of the land and calls it "Crown land," even if the Crown did not have money to buy it.

The Commissioner went on to say, "We want to use some of your land so that our people can make a living off of farming." The Commissioner told our Chiefs and Peoples that the settlers wanted to use our land "to the depth of a plough." The concept of "the depth of a plough" was brought to the Cree Peoples by the Commissioner. Cree Peoples did not farm. The concept of the depth of a plough came from the Crown's Treaty Commissioner. Let us be clear: the Treaty Commissioner wanted to use the land to the depth of a plough. There was no request for anything below that depth. The resources below the surface, which this concept does not cover, were taken by the colonizers without Indigenous Peoples' consent.

Treaty Rights

Let us review the Treaty in the context of rights for each side of the treaty-making. Most discussions fail to mention the treaty rights of non-indigenous people. This is a critical issue. In a treaty relationship, there are two sides and both have rights. Non-indigenous historians and other scholars fail to educate their own people on their rights under the treaties. If you stopped ten people to ask, "What are your treaty rights?" most of them would consider the question irrelevant. "Treaty, what's that?" Every non-indigenous person should know his or her treaty rights. The simple fact is that, without the treaty, no one other than Indigenous Peoples has the right to live in our land. The International Court of Justice in the *Western Sahara* case stated that the only way for non-indigenous people to live in the lands of Indigenous Peoples is through a treaty. Everyone who has come to live on Great Turtle Island since contact is living here as a result of a treaty. To discount the treaty or deny the treaty rights of non-indigenous people is to make illegitimate foreign people's occupancy of Great Turtle Island.

What are the treaty rights of non-indigenous people? The primary right is that non-indigenous people can live in our lands. Indigenous Peoples honour that right; they are not interfering with the treaty rights of non-indigenous people. Indigenous Peoples are not walking into the homes of non-indigenous people, opening their fridges, taking food out and eating it. If an Indigenous person did that, he or she could be charged under non-indigenous law with break-and-enter. The reverse, however, is not true. Non-indigenous people have no problem with hunting our animals, taking our fish and our birds. The Commissioner told the Indigenous Peoples in 1876 that the settlers would not need these things, so he did not request that the Cree Peoples extend these rights to the settlers. Therefore, it is not a treaty right to take these things. Yet the settlers continue to violate the treaty in this way.

The question remains: what are the treaty rights of the non-indigenous people? Our Elders agreed that rights could be given to the non-indigenous people coming into our lands. At the time of the treaty-making, the Treaty Commissioner's people said to our people, "We want to live here in peace." This is a treaty right. When non-indigenous people think that their land rights are being violated, they react. They do not see that the right to live in peace is a two-way street. Look at Oka, when Mohawk Peoples said, "We do not want you building a golf course on our cemetery." The Mohawks asked the non-indigenous people to respect those who have passed to the spirit world. In response, non-indigenous people sent in the military—just as they did at Gustafson Lake, when the Indigenous Peoples said, "Don't interfere with our Sun Dance ground." Do Indigenous Peoples react like this, with violence? The Elders always say, "We said that we would let them live in peace." This has a meaning for Cree Peoples. The Elders say, "Honour that treaty we made. We gave our word at the time of the treaty-making that we would let them live in peace in our land." These are the living treaty rights by which we live every day. They are rights that the Elders gave to the Treaty Commissioner, as they were requested. However, the Treaty Commissioner did a poor job conveying the treaty to the colonizing government and to the settlers.

In 1876, the Treaty Commissioner also said, "Our people over there have nothing, they have no place to live; they're poor with very little to eat, their children are dying. Let us bring them over here so that they can live and be healthy; and let us use some of the resources of your land, some of the wood to build houses, so they can put great crops in the ground to grow things for themselves. Let us use some of the hay for their animals." And the Indigenous Peoples, feeling pity for those poor people, said, "Okay, we will let you do that." The first time that I travelled to Europe, I was shocked by what I saw. I expected to see slums and sewers running into streets because of what the Elders were told about how Europeans lived. I was surprised when I saw great buildings and clean roads. People were not starving on the streets in London, Paris, or Amsterdam. When we were growing up, the stories of the horrible conditions in which Europeans lived were shocking to us—but they made the treaty understandable. The Treaty Commissioner had told us that this was why his people wanted to live in our lands. Our people pitied them and said, "Okay, they are living like that; no human being should be allowed to live like that. They can live in our land. They can use some of our resources, some of the water, some of the wood, some of the ground, so that they can live." Sharing our resources, a treaty right of non-indigenous peoples, has led to the colonizing government assuming control over all the resources above and below the surface. This is a treaty violation. One of the main treaty rights of the non-indigenous person is to respect the land. This is not being done. Our lands are being destroyed by the non-indigenous people. Our animals, our birds, our fish, and all living things are disappearing. The ones that are left behind are suffering. This rich land is being destroyed.This is a violation of the treaty by the non-indigenous people. The non-indigenous people are forgetting to have respect for the land and all its relationships.

Who Would Give Away so Much?

At the time of the treaty-making, it was the Indigenous Peoples who had the upper hand in the treaty negotiations. If you listen to the way the Elders tell it—as I have listened to them—the Elders at treaty-making told the Treaty Commissioners, "We are not selling our land. We cannot sell our land. This land belongs to us. We can let you use some of our land but we will not sell our land. We have a relationship with the land. The Creation placed us here on Great Turtle Island and this is our land. However, we will let you live in our land."

If you listen to the non-indigenous people and read their papers, it's a different story. The non-indigenous people tell us, "Look, it is written down. Peoples ceded, surrendered, and released the land to the colonizers." When you read between the lines, the papers suggest that Indigenous Peoples gave up to the colonizers our governments, our legal systems, our children, our life. This is not honouring treaties made in "good faith." These are lies written on paper and voiced by governments and academics. Lies written on paper are not true for anyone.

Now, seriously, what kind of people would agree to give up these things? There are five thousand Indigenous Peoples camped at Fort Carlton. There are thirty non-indigenous people sitting at the treaty table in their red uniforms, saying, "You put your pen to this paper and you give up everything." Be logical: does that make any sense? Yet, over and over, government officials say to us, "You gave up everything. You gave up the land, you gave up your law, and you gave up your government."

Even in this century, the non-indigenous government of Canada says, "We will give you a government that we will call self-government." What is our response? "The Creation gave us a government. How can you give us a government? Did the Creation pass on and make you the new Creation?" There is some kind of weird idea operating here: somehow, the treaty-making made Indigenous Peoples and our entire way of living subservient to the colonizers and their institutions. Rather than acknowledge that the treaties mean something to all the Peoples living in our territories, the government of Canada has consistently tried to downgrade the treaties and our governments that made those treaties.[13] Why would Indigenous Peoples want a version of a government that does not seem to work for its own people? Why would an Indigenous nation with a governing process in place before the colonizers came here take on a structure that does not seem to work? Under the treaty, we were to live side by side, to co-exist peacefully on our lands.[14] This is the meaning of the treaty for Indigenous Peoples.

Assimilation Policy: Getting Rid of the Treaties?

In 1969, Jean Chrétien, then Minister of Indian Affairs, came out with a "white paper" that outlined a policy to do away with Indigenous Peoples' rights and reserved lands. The theory behind this white paper was simple: Indigenous Peoples no longer needed their lands and should assimilate into Canadian society. It was not a new idea, but about the sixth such plan that the colonizer had attempted. The first prime minister of Canada, John A. Macdonald—also a minister of Indian Affairs—wanted to eliminate "Indians" by 1896. A later government revised the date to 1920, and then 1950, and then 1970. Chrétien's 1969 white paper basically said that Canada hoped to be rid of "Indians" by the year 2000. I guess we're hanging on a tenuous edge here, trying to exist as distinct Peoples when the state of Canada wants to get rid of us so badly.[15]

One of the "Indian" things that Canada wants to get rid of is the treaties. I can understand that. But Canada is a successor state and not the nation that made the treaties with our nations. Canada is a Johnny-come-lately to the process. Canada could not make international treaties until the Statute of Westminster in 1932; before that date, Mother England made all the treaties on behalf of Canada. A Treaty Commissioner representing the Crown concluded the treaties with our nations, and Canada inherited those treaty obligations and responsibilities from Mother

England. It is Canada's obligation to implement the commitments made under those treaties. Canada may want to rid itself of those treaties, but Canada possesses no legal right to change them. This fact has been asserted in recent law.

In 1980–81, while Canada was trying to achieve constitutional independence from Mother England, Indigenous Peoples stirred up some dust in the English courts and the halls of Westminster. The court case, called *The Indian Association of Alberta* v. *the Foreign and Commonwealth Secretary*, went all the way to the House of Lords, the highest court in England. This was a really critical court case for a couple of reasons. First, no legal firm in Canada would touch the case. The Indian Association of Alberta went looking for legal council for assistance in mounting a case in England. The late Sam Bull, Wallace Manyfingers, and I went to law firms in Vancouver, Toronto, Montreal—you name them; we went to talk to them. And they all told us, "You're nuts; you cannot go to court in England. You have no standing to appear before the Courts in England." But the Elders said, "Go, because the treaties are important. We made treaties with Mother England, and it must mean something." So we found lawyers in England who were prepared to take the case and we did get into court. We did have standing before the courts in England because of the treaties made in the 1870s. And Indigenous Peoples won this case at a number of levels. We learned not to believe the lawyers trained in the law schools of colonial Canada, since they don't know enough about our treaties.

The second important thing to remember about the case is that the Court of Appeal decision and findings were not overturned by the British House of Lords. Lord Denning's judgment for the Court of Appeal stated that "No parliament or legislature can change the Treaty without the consent of the Treaty Peoples."[16] Because this decision was handed down before the parliament at Westminster patriated the British North America Act of 1867 to Canada, the court's decision came with the Constitution of Canada. No parliament can change our treaties without our consent, although they have tried to do so. The *Indian Association* case is an important aid to Indigenous Peoples fighting for our treaty rights.

At the time of the 1969 white paper, the Elders saw the path that Canada wanted to follow: Canada wanted the treaties gone. I have no problem with that; I say to people who take that position, "Okay, fine, pack up your duds and get on the first boat out of here. If there are any trees left, cut them down, build yourself a raft, and ship out." If there are no treaties, the colonizers have no legitimate right to be on our lands. Canada would become an international pariah under international law, akin to South Africa or Rhodesia when they declared unilateral independence. Without the treaties, what legitimate law can the colonizers use to occupy our lands?

If Canada gets rid of the treaties, what happens to the treaty rights of the non-indigenous people? Those rights to live in peace in our lands and share our resources become null and void. The logical conclusion to terminating our treaties—if that were legally possible—is that the non-indigenous people would have to vacate our territories. Perhaps Canadians need to spend more time thinking about their treaty rights and telling their government to honour the obligations that give them so many benefits.

Instead, the successor state and its institutions are complicit in trying to downgrade the treaties and the treaty-making process; government officials refer to them as "domestic" treaties. Colonization persists to this day, as the idea that treaties do not matter is still taught in many universities. It is in the interests of mainstream institutions to perpetuate these false foundations. Many professors still teach students that treaties with Indigenous Peoples are not relevant, that they cannot be recognized because there is only one sovereign entity in Canada. As a doctoral student, I was shocked and offended when the chair of a political science department told me who the only sovereign in Canada is. I said, "The Cree?" And she said, "No, Canada is the only legitimate sovereign entity and the sooner Indigenous Peoples accept that the better off they will be." Well, being a Cree woman, I refused to accept that position. Our Elders who made the treaty did not pass to the spirit world with lies on their lips. When those Elders said that we never sold the land at the time of the treaty-making, I am not going to say that we did. When those Elders said that we have our own government and our own legal system, it is not up to me to deny that. I do not care how much pressure the colonizers put us under to change our minds. There are many sovereign entities of Great Turtle Island—not one, not the state of Canada. The Indigenous nations are sovereign.

As a doctoral student in political science, I was told that Indigenous history and political history did not factor into discussions about these treaties. The only acceptable academic perspective was from within the Canadian legal framework. Academics constrained me from speaking from an Indigenous perspective. I would have had to assimilate or adopt a mainstream position. To hold to Indigenous perspectives and beliefs, I had to leave the institution and not complete my degree at that university.

The United Nations Recognizes our Treaties
Because of pressure exerted by Indigenous Peoples, Chrétien's 1969 white paper policy was put on the shelf and we got some breathing room.

However, the Elders were not convinced that Canada was going to stop its policies to get rid of the treaties and Indigenous Peoples. The Elders told us, "We can't trust these guys. Definitely, we cannot trust the state of Canada to protect our treaties and our lands and territories. Indigenous Peoples have to do something to protect the lands and resources that were protected under the terms of the treaty. Indigenous Peoples cannot depend on the state of Canada to live up to the honour of the Crown and the obligations and responsibilities of the Crown. These Canadian people are not honourable." As a result, the Elders sent a delegation from Alberta and Saskatchewan to the United Nations in 1974 to find an avenue to protect the treaties.

Going to the United Nations in 1974 started a long process in which we established our identity and status as Indigenous Peoples in international law. Indigenous Peoples were not on the horizon and did not figure into the politics of the UN. Many officials at the UN, thinking Indigenous Peoples were extinct, asked, "Didn't Columbus wipe out the Indigenous Peoples in America?" Well, yes, but despite the attempts at genocide, we are still kicking. I describe the efforts of Indigenous Peoples to organize at the UN and to gain recognition in my book *Our Elders Understand Our Rights*. The main reason that Indigenous Peoples went to the UN was to focus attention on our treaties. It is important to understand that nations make treaties. Individuals do not make treaties. The UN is the body that deals with international legal norms. Our treaty needed to have the attention of the UN because there were all kinds of problems in Canada with the recognition and implementation of the treaties as understood by our Chiefs and Elders. Indigenous Peoples wanted the UN to help us have the treaties recognized as international instruments and to assist Indigenous Peoples with the implementation of those treaties. Indigenous Peoples are organized into nations, and nations, according to the articles of the Charter of the UN, have a right of self-determination.[17] In addition, there are laws under the Vienna Convention on Treaties that apply to treaties between nations, but state governments argue that Indigenous treaties are not covered by the Convention. It was therefore necessary to do a study on treaties, but in order to get a study a forum first needed to be created to bring a resolution to do a study.

This was a long process since Indigenous Peoples had been excluded from the formation of the UN. The Indigenous Peoples lobbied and pushed for the creation of the Working Group on Indigenous Peoples (WGIP). In 1982, the WGIP was created with a mandate to conduct studies. Then, a resolution needed to be moved through the system to get the study. It took until May 1989 for the UN to agree to a study on treaties. The importance of the vote to accept to do a study on treaties made by Indigenous Peoples was that the UN accepted jurisdiction. That our treaties meant something in international law was a giant victory for Indigenous Peoples. To have a study was the first step towards recognition. Although the UN was unsure of its exact status, the purpose of the study was to determine the international nature of our treaties. It took that intensive lobbying from 1974 until 1989. We never gave up. The UN started the study that took until 1999 to complete. The UN did eventually become convinced that our treaties are international treaties.

To enter into a treaty, a party must be a nation. A colonizer is not a nation. When I was lobbying at the United Nations in the 1980s, the colonizers frequently stated that Indigenous treaties were not "real" treaties within international law. Canada's diplomatic staff told UN staff and other governments that Canada uses that word "Treaty" because it makes the Indigenous Peoples feel that they are participating in a seemingly equitable and reciprocal process. This explanation held no water at the UN. According to a UN-approved study on treaties, the concept that the treaties were not "real" was without international validity—just as the concept of apartheid is not a valid one.[18]

In 1989, the United Nations appointed a Special Rapporteur, Miguel Alfonso Martinez, to undertake a study of the treaties of Indigenous Peoples. Martinez looked at treaties not only in Canada but also in the United States, New Zealand, Hawaii, Chile (the Mapuche), and elsewhere. It is important to point out that the Special Rapporteur was an independent legal expert. He is not from North America. He had not been educated in a colonizer's system. Dr. Martinez looked at the legal issues and treaties independently and from an international legal perspective. Dr. Martinez made a lot of important findings in his progress reports and in his final report, which he submitted in 1999. His final report states, "In the course of history, the newcomers [i.e., colonizers/settlers]...attempted to divest Indigenous Peoples...of their sovereign attributes, especially jurisdiction over their lands, recognition of their forms of societal organization, and their status as subjects of international law."[19] Dr. Martinez examined and explicitly condemned the unwillingness of colonizers to uphold the rights and status of Indigenous Peoples.

The United Nations has accepted the Special Rapporteur's report on treaties. The legal experts on the Sub-commission on Prevention of Discrimination and the Protection of Minorities received his report with praise. After ten years of study, Dr. Martinez concluded that the treaties "indeed continue to maintain their original status, and [are] fully in effect and consequently are sources of rights and obligations for all the original parties to them and their successors who shall fulfill their provisions in good faith."[20] The Special Rapporteur concluded that the treaties negotiated in North America and other parts of the world are in fact international treaties, and that Indigenous nations are subjects of international law. After five hundred years of colonization, Indigenous Peoples were found to be not *objects* but *subjects* of international law. Finally, the UN Special Rapporteur concluded that these treaties need to be honoured by the original signatory nations and their successors, such as Canada.

Treaty Process in Canada?

Indigenous Peoples have found that there is no process in Canada to deal with our treaties because the state of Canada has no will to honour them. If state officials do not like the way Indigenous Peoples pursue claims under our treaties, they manipulate their own guidelines to stop or subvert the process. Indigenous Peoples can find no justice within Canada for bad faith or lack of commitment to our treaties. Indigenous Peoples need an international mechanism to assist in the implementation of our treaties. A treaty violation by the state of Canada should be dealt with at an international tribunal, where Canada will have to answer for not honouring treaty obligations. The United Nations is working on such a process. In December 2003, the United Nations Commission on Human Rights, through the office of the High Commissioner for Human Rights, met in Geneva to follow up on the *Study on Treaties, Agreements and other Constructive Arrangements between States and Indigenous Peoples.* This Commission affirmed the need for the treaties to be "understood and implemented in accordance with the spirit in which they were agreed upon."[21] The report was presented to the Working Group on Indigenous Peoples during its session in July 2004, and includes a programme of action for the United Nations and its different bodies to act on for the implementation of the *Study on Treaties, Agreements and other Constructive Arrangements between States and Indigenous Peoples.* Following this report, the United Nations, through the office of the High Commissioner for Human Rights, was mandated by the Economic and Social Council to hold a seminar to follow up on the *Study on Treaties.* This seminar is scheduled to take place within the Treaty Six Territory[22] of Great Turtle Island on 15–17 November 2006. One of the topics to be covered is the work needed to be undertaken for the implementation of the treaties by the United Nations.[23]

This is a big change for Indigenous Peoples. In 1974, the UN did not know that we existed and still took care of our territories. Now, the UN is coming to our territories to hear from our Peoples. As with the treaty-making, the effort is being made to come to our homelands. It is a sign of the times. It is a sign of respect for Indigenous Peoples and our Nations.

Indigenous Peoples will not continue to be discounted in our own territories. The Creation placed us on our territories to take care of this land—not only for ourselves but also for the future generations. Indigenous Peoples cannot give up that responsibility because to do so would be to discount our relationship with the Creation. The colonizers have to acknowledge their treaty rights in order to continue living in our lands. They live here because we let them live here—there is no other reason. This is the meaning of the treaty from our point of view.

NOTES

1 For more information, see Sharon H. Venne (ed.), "Understanding Treaty Six: An Indigenous Perspective"; Sharon H. Venne (ed.), *Honour Bound: Onion Lake and the Spirit of Treaty Six—The International Validity of Treaties with Indigenous Peoples*; and Sharon H. Venne (ed.), "Treaty Doubletalk in Canada."

2 Editor's Note: When I asked Sharon Venne about her preference for using the English word "Creation" rather than the more familiar "Creator," which she had used in earlier drafts, Sharon explained, "I changed Creator to the Creation as an Elder told me that it was wrong to refer to a single being as a creator rather than to the bigger picture of the Creation—basically—Indigenous Peoples are a bit brainwashed by the idea of a single 'god' rather than to see that male and female are jointly responsible for life—all life—so it is the Creation—which is a more reflective position of our Indigenous world view" (E-mail to author, 13 Sept. 2006).

3 The earliest policies of the administration in British North America were designed to contain the "Indians." Augie Fleras and Jean Leonard Elliott observe that "Many [Indians] were herded onto reserves for protection from lawless elements interested only in profit and amusement" (41). See also Tanner 16–17.

4 For more information on the history of Papaschase Cree, see Dwayne Trevor Donald, "Edmonton Pentimento: Re-Reading History in the case of Papaschase Cree."

5 *Rose Lameman, Francis Saulteaux, Nora Alook et al. v. Attorney General of Canada* (2004), Alberta Court of Queen's Bench 665, par. 35.

6 In February 2001, the descendants of Papaschase filed legal action against Canada for breach of treaty, and for fiduciary, statutory, and trust obligations owed to the Papaschase Peoples. Part of the action asked the court to review the validity of the reserve surrender and the breach of the surrender trust agreement. This legal action was dismissed by Justice Frans F. Slatter on 13 September 2004. See previous note for citation. In an appeal decision handed down at the Alberta Court of Appeal on December 19, 2006, Papaschase Peoples were given leave to have their case heard in court.

7 According to the Vienna Convention on the Law of Treaties, a treaty is an agreement freely entered into in good faith between two or more sovereign entities designed to express their intentions for future relations. This is a paraphrase of the Vienna Convention on the Law of Treaties (1969), 1155, United Nations Treaty Series 331, in force 27 January 1980.

8 On 18 May 2006, Oren Lyons, Faithkeeper of the Onondaga Nation (Haudenosaunee),
   spoke at the Permanent Forum on Indigenous Peoples held at the United Nations Building
   in New York City. In a discussion as to why the papal bulls need to be revoked, Mr. Lyons
   provided a lyrical ancestral memory of life on Turtle Island B.C.—"before Columbus"—as a
   pristine land of plenty where "peace was prevalent" because everyone understood the basic
   unwritten law that is the foundation of peace: respect for each other and for the land. Lyons
   said, "Then our brother came from across the water, and my grandmother said it was like a
   black cloud rolling towards us, a rolling black cloud coming at us, and it covered us. That's
   how she described it." According to Lyons, the two sides have "different ideas," so that
   "even in today's dialogue we still don't quite connect because we're on a different spiritual
   level. They don't quite understand [the meaning of] relationship. We never gave up our
   relations with the earth." See the Indigenous Law Institute website at www.ili.nativeweb.org/
   ictarticl.html, and also the question and answer section at the end of this book, pp. 79–97,
   for further discussion of the papal bulls.

9 For more information on the international status of Indigenous peoples and the legal
   necessity for treaty-making to access the lands and resources of Indigenous peoples, see
   Miguel Alfonso Martinez, Special Rapporteur, UN Doc., *Study on Treaties, Agreements and Other
   Constructive Arrangements Between States and Indigenous Populations*, First Progress Report, E/
   CN.4/Sub.2/1992/31; *Study on Treaties, Agreements and Other Constructive Arrangements Between
   States and Indigenous Populations*, Second Progress Report, E/CN.4/Sub.2/1995/27; *Study on
   Treaties, Agreements and Other Constructive Arrangements Between States and Indigenous Populations*,
   Third Progress Report, E/CN.4/Sub.2/1996/23; and *Study on Treaties, Agreements and Other
   Constructive Arrangements Between States and Indigenous Populations*, Final Report, E/CN.4/
   Sub.2/1999/20. For additional reading in the area of treaties and their international status,
   see Isabelle Schulte-Tenckhoff, 239.

10 *Western Sahara: Advisory Opinion* [1975], International Court of Justice Reports 12. See also
   chapter 2 in Sharon H. Venne, *Our Elders Understand our Rights: Evolving International Law
   Regarding Indigenous Peoples*.

11 As evidenced by the Royal Proclamation of 1763.

12 These words are a translation of the words used by the Elders.

13 Readers who believe that such misreprepresentations of the meaning of treaties do not
   continue to occur in our own time might consider a document recently released by the
   Saskatchewan government, which contains the following introduction to treaty rights: "Treaty
   rights are the rights that First Nations have as a result of special agreements entered into with
   Canada. In Canadian law, these Treaties are unique: they are not international agreement"
   (*Government of Saskatchewan Guidelines for Consultation with First Nations and Metis People: A Guide
   for Decision Makers*, May 2006). First of all, the treaties under discussion are international
   agreements as found by the United Nations in their study. The treaties were made with the
   Crown and not with Canada. This is how history is distorted and leads to disrespect.

14 For more information, see Oren Lyons (ed.), *Exiled in the Land of the Free: Democracy, Indian
   Nations, and the U.S. Constitution*.

15 There has been a lot of press recently regarding Canada's failure on June 29, 2006, to
   support the Declaration on the Rights of Indigenous Peoples during the debates at the newly
   created Human Rights Council. The United Nations Human Rights Council adopted the
   Declaration in an "embarrassing defeat for Canada." Only two countries, Canada and Russia,
   voted against this Declaration. It should not be a surprise to anyone, however, that Canada
   voted against the Declaration. The state has been actively trying to kill the draft since it was
   first discussed in the United Nations in the 1980s. The Canadian delegates have tried various
   tactics over the years to subvert the declaration, just as they attempted to stop the UN study
   on treaties.

16 *The Indian Association of Alberta v. the Foreign and Commonwealth Secretary* (1983). All England Reports.

17 Supra, note 9, 71–74.

18 Supra, note 8.

19 Supra, note 8 at par. 112 of the final report by the Special Rapporteur.

20 Supra, note 8, at par. 271 of the final report by the Special Rapporteur.

21 E/CN. 4/2004/111 and par. 2.

22 For those who are unfamiliar with the Treaty Six Territory, it is in present western Canada from the Rocky Mountains to Manitoba. The Seminar is scheduled for Samson Cree Territory, near Hobbema, Alberta.

23 The UN Seminar will cover the following themes: Indigenous understanding of treaties and consideration of the meaning of constructive arrangements; free, prior, and informed consent as it relates to treaties; implementing treaties and treaty rights, with examples of good practices from around the world; development of effective mechanisms at all levels to defend and uphold treaty tights; the UN and OAS Declarations and Treaty Rights; current work and next steps at the international level to monitor and enforce reaties, agreements, and constructive arrangements.

TWO

THREE TREATY NATIONS COMPARED

Economic and Political Consequences for Indigenous People in Canada, the United States, and New Zealand

Patricia Seed

INITIALLY ENGLISH COLONISTS could legally gain possession of indigenous lands in the New World merely by building fences, houses, and gardens. Such actions, however, could only secure a restricted territory, limited by the physical property boundaries. Furthermore, these activities only secured rights for individuals rather than for states. After the mid-seventeenth century, English officials became increasingly active in dispossessions. Lacking the ability physically to surround the entire territory they wished to command, colonial officials turned to a different method of expropriation that they called "treaties." While today we have a very clear idea of what constitutes a treaty, English colonial officials were in fact employing a culturally unique instrument in pursuit of native land—using cultural and linguistic assumptions not characteristic of other European colonial powers.[1]

By the start of the eighteenth century, officials regularly seized native land through this proceeding in the three English overseas colonies that became the United States, Canada, and New Zealand. As a result, indigenous communities today in these three contemporary nations must all employ the language of treaties in order to gain legitimate hearings for their grievances.

In arguing for restitution of land rights, however, these three treaty nations have encountered nationally distinct twentieth- and twenty-first-century interpretations of these earlier accords. Because each of these former English colonies—Canada, the United States, and New Zealand—considers its own viewpoint on these agreements as unassailably correct, each customarily fails to look beyond its own borders to see how its enforcement of indigenous people's treaties stands up against that of other former English colonies.[2] Such comparisons illustrate a considerable range of interpretations and differing roadblocks that indigenous communities have encountered.

In order to understand how these currently important features function, we will first describe the shared history of English colonial objectives and the culturally distinctive historical understanding of "treaty."

English-speaking colonists for centuries have, for reasons lying deep in England's past, sought land as the central economic goal of overseas colonization. In the Middle Ages, writes William Holdsworth, "land law was the most important and the most highly developed branch of the common law" (145). The eminent legal historian F.F.C. Milsom observes that the first legal textbook in England in 1496 dealt with land law, adding that it was nearly four centuries before textbooks were written on other branches of law (3–4). The foundation of the English legal system lay in the ownership of soil, a trend that would be extended wherever Englishmen settled overseas. In English law at the time, the early moments of colonization, only the monarch enjoyed full dominion over the land and hence ultimate authority for control over it. Queen Elizabeth's letters patent, the first official legal acts of English sovereignty over the New World, established this pattern. Sir Humphrey Gilbert and Walter Ralegh were entitled to "have, hold, occupy, and enjoy all the *soil* of such lands, countries, and territories." It was soil in places that Gilbert and Ralegh received the right to hold and enjoy. As Gilbert's and Ralegh's patents both state, these lands were granted "with the full power to dispose thereof and in every part in fee simple or otherwise according to the laws of England." In other words, the land of the New World was given to use and distribute according to "the laws of England" (Hakluyt 8:18).

Land ownership constituted not merely the official, but also the cultural, heart of the English invention of America as theirs, undivided by class. Aspiring to own land in the New World cut across social ranks and constituted a socially desirable practice for all individuals, as well as a worthy public goal. Members of the upper classes as well as landless farmers could legitimately aspire to own the soil of the New World.

And when early colonial critics attacked their country's land expropriation policies, they limited themselves to criticizing the means but not the ends of land acquisition. Roger Williams criticized the Royal Letters Patent and the popular Puritan belief in the eminent domain of English agriculture, arguing *only* for a different process of acquiring native lands. Similarly, William Penn altered the means but, again, not the ends of English colonization in the Americas (Kent 9–10; Williams 1:120).

But other unique features of English colonization of land existed. Alone among the Western European traditions, early seventeenth-century English law did not require a written procedure for claiming ownership of land. Until near the end of the seventeenth century, Englishmen could claim that they had acquired ownership of land simply by exchanging other commodities for it and by performing physical labour upon it. Therefore, unlike all other Europeans, English colonists overseas understood actions such as handing over money, building a house, putting up fences, and planting crops, which they customarily called labour, as establishing individual legal dominion over a terrain—just as it had in England. Such belief in the transparent meaning of particular actions, without benefit of either a speech or a written document, made it possible for hundreds of illiterate or barely literate Englishmen to acquire plots of land at the start of colonization (Seed).

In one other significant way, however, Englishmen shared a similar approach to other European colonizers. In all overseas possessions, colonizers (or their theorists at home) created a dividing line between humanity and quasi-humanity, separating colonizers from the natives. In describing the quasi-humanity of natives, colonists frequently employed animal metaphors. These images constitute what I call the colonial fiction of the not-quite-human aboriginal. Colonists from all European legal traditions invoked this distinction, but their fictions differed, for politically and culturally specific reasons.

The English colonial fiction of indigenous people centred on the image of the hunter who lacks a real home, having only animal-like "sties and dens" for housing (Mather 88). In this fictionalized depiction, natives simply cavorted on the land, chasing game across grass and meadows. The choice of this representation in the English colonial tradition of native as an almost-animal hunter was far from random. According to the very complicated history of English law and Norman law, even human hunters did not actually own the land on which they hunted. Hunting rights over land, in other words, were separable from land ownership. And under English law, only farmers had that right to own the land, not hunters. Thus began the English colonial fiction that all natives were hunters because hunting did not entitle them as individuals to legal ownership (Seed).

While a fiction is always a fiction, a colonial fiction remains a fixed idea despite overwhelming evidence that it is wrong. When the Cherokees were pushed out of the US state of Georgia in the 1830s, many were growing cotton on huge plantations. Obviously, they were not hunters—but the colonial fiction overrode the reality even in the writings of the judges. In their decision Supreme Court justices insisted these agricultural Cherokees were "hunters" (McLoughlin). To admit the reality of native farming would have meant acknowledging legitimate Cherokee ownership of land because in the English legal tradition the mere act of farming created legitimate ownership. Hence, in this and similar collisions between truth and fiction, fiction won, because admitting reality would have threatened settlers' desire to perceive themselves as acting legitimately when taking away land from Native Americans.

Other European settlers, however, behaved no better, only establishing their own separate colonial fictions. Spanish and Portuguese colonists, for example, created representations of indigenous people to pursue a different colonial economic objective, labour, rather than land (Seed).

While colonial fictions culturally satisfied Europeans and their successor citizens that they were justified in displacing or using the native inhabitants, fictions alone did not legitimate their actions. In the previous essay, Sharon Venne rightly stresses the importance of legal title to English occupation—a fact often overlooked in studies of colonization. In English law, the actions of farming or "improving" land actually created legal title for the individual performing these acts. But when English officials sought to exercise greater control over the process—and acquire dominion over larger tracts of land than an individual could control—they instituted a more formal written mechanism of expropriation.

Beginning in the second half of the eighteenth century and continuing into the following century, in Canada, as well as in the United States and New Zealand, a written document became increasingly common as the formal legal device for obtaining indigenous land. This document was denominated a "treaty," a legal form with a distinctly English flavour. To understand this distinctiveness, however, we need to understand the history of the word itself.

The word "treaty" in English has an historically distinctive meaning compared to other European languages. In the Romance (Latin-derived) European languages and some Germanic ones as well, "treaty" derives from a word meaning to deal with a person face to face. In Spanish, Portuguese, Dutch, and French, the word comes from the verb "to treat," meaning to relate to or deal with someone personally.[3] A treaty was thus something arranged in person, as opposed to communicated anonymously. Treaties, therefore, could only result from direct personal contact between one group and another.

While many European colonizers signed written accords with native peoples, these agreements frequently had other goals. Spanish treaties with indigenous people primarily sought protection for their own trade goods and internal communication. By the end of the sixteenth century, after major native empires had surrendered, Spaniards increasingly encountered powerful native groups who practised guerilla strategies. Realizing that full-scale continued war was a fruitless effort and protection for caravans of trade goods and people extremely expensive, Spanish officials signed agreements with native people to ensure the continued flow of goods and services through regions dominated by hostile tribes. They termed these safe passage pacts "treaties."

Portuguese and then later Dutch officials used treaties with aboriginal people principally to manage commercial relations—to acquire everything from sugar to shellac (Biker). In these arrangements, control over commerce fell under governmental (Portuguese) or semi-governmental (Dutch) purview. Following in the footsteps of the Portuguese and the Dutch in both Africa and Asia, British and French trading companies (not their governments) subsequently imitated these trade agreements.

While English officials arranged treaties in similar circumstances as the Spanish, Portuguese, and Dutch—at the cessation of hostilities and to acquire beaver skins, canoes, or other trade goods—English treaties often contained an additional objective, unique to their political system, namely the relinquishment of native land. This requirement for land surrender rarely appeared in any of the treaties of other nations, but it dominates the English language treaties with indigenous people.

While signifying a discussion of terms or negotiations in English, and English alone of the Western European languages, the word "treaty" also signified *writing*. From the fourteenth century, when the word first appeared in English, until the middle of the seventeenth century, "treaty" primarily meant a form of inscription: a story, narrative, written account, treating a subject in writing. As a result, any *written* agreement between two English subjects could and indeed was called a treaty, not just an agreement between states (*Oxford English Dictionary*). Hence, while the earliest written agreements between English colonists and Native Americans were called treaties, at the time this word simply referred to the fact that the agreement (between individuals) was written down. The 1621 pact between Massasoit, leader of the Pokanoket near the Plymouth colony, was labelled a treaty at the time. But that word does not necessarily mean an accord between nations or political authorities but only an agreement written on paper (Morton 24).

This later (eighteenth and subsequent centuries) interpretation of treaties as written agreements had important consequences for native peoples everywhere. Showing such partiality for written accords demonstrated a disregard for the power of oral tradition in the native communities as well as for any verbal agreement between U.S. or Canadian officials and an indigenous community.

When native communities protested the lack of correspondence between the oral agreement and the written text, British colonial and later American officials instead invoked their own recently developed (late seventeenth-century) legal rules, which rendered oral agreements often worthless and always gave the written text of an agreement priority over an oral one (Holdsworth 122). In 1793, Oneida leaders complained of this deceptive practice: "We return home after treaty negotiations possessed with an idea that we had leased our country to the people of the state, reserving a rent which was to increase with the increase of settlements on our lands, and then remaining a rent forever. This was our idea of the matter. We supposed at the time that we had reserved a sufficient tract of the country for our own cultivation, but since we had time to consult the writings and have them properly explained and seen the proceedings of your surveyors, we find our hopes and expectations blasted and disappointed in every particular. Instead of leasing our country to you for a respectable rent, we find that we have ceded and granted it forever for the consideration of the inconsiderable sum of six hundred dollars a year" (Hough 1:360–61).

This shift to an official written instrument to gain legal title to indigenous land occurred in the three colonial regions that became the United States, Canada, and New Zealand. Beyond the shift to written documents in legal culture, government officials had three different reasons for beginning the treaty process. First, they obtained greater political control over the process of acquisition of land. When individuals could independently establish claims (as they did in the early years of US settlement), lawsuits inevitably followed. Limiting land acquisition to political officials and enabling them to dispense new land grants tamped down the earlier squabbles among colonists.

This system had a second advantage over the earlier method, namely the political standing of the signatories. Unlike agreements between private individuals, agreements with government representatives as signatories created a politically more secure claim on indigenous territories.

Finally, the practices surrounding the written treaties differed notably in their ceremonial aspect from previous popular English legitimating strategies of land acquisition. Building houses and fences were activities lacking in ritual content. Negotiations and signing treaty purchases of land often included elements of indigenous ceremonies: circulating peace pipes, lengthy speeches, and even proper decorum during speeches. In all three treaty nations elaborate rituals accompanied formal signings of treaties that placed control over land redistribution in colonial and post-colonial governments' hands.

But incorporating native rituals into the treaty signings did not occur out of respect, but as a means of coercing native leaders retroactively to accept terms that were not clearly spelled out orally at signing. Governor Clinton of New York state reminded the natives of "smoking our pipes together" when insisting that they had to abide by the terms of a written agreement totally at odds with the one they had verbally agreed to sign (Hough 1:355).

The most unique of all the treaties British colonial officials signed was in New Zealand. While in Canada and the United States such agreements were only signed in the English language, leaving the interpretation solely up to a single signatory, in New Zealand the Treaty of Waitangi, signed between the British Crown and the Maori in 1840, is bilingual. In other words, both a Maori version and an English version were composed at the time of signing. A record therefore exists of the accord that nineteenth-century Maori leaders agreed to.

In the 1980s, a legendary Maori attorney, Sir Hugh Kawharu, painstakingly retranslated the Maori version. Not surprisingly, his translation of the Maori text does not entirely accord with the official English publication also composed in 1840 (Kawharu). According to the Maori-language version of the treaty, native peoples ceded something called *raratanga* to the English. What is *raratanga*? In Maori, *raratanga* consists of a kind of authority, but it encompasses all authority over neither the islands nor all of its resources (Walker). The English version declares that the Maori have granted something else. In English, the Maori cede sovereignty (i.e. all authority) over *land* to the Crown. Having a bilingual treaty has opened the door for the Maori to enter into legal debates and sometimes lengthy negotiation. In New Zealand more than three decades of discussion have ensued over what exactly was meant by *raratanga* at the time the treaty was signed and precisely what, if any, other natural resources the Maori ceded in this treaty besides land (Maaka and Fleras; Pocock, "Law," 486; Orange; Sharp).

Having a bilingual treaty, however, would have remained irrelevant had it not been for the decision of the New Zealand government in 1975 that the treaty was binding on the government and that Maori had a right to seek redress for violations of its provisions. The bilaterally binding status of the Treaty of Waitangi contrasts with the legal standing of treaties with natives in the United States this past century. Readers might be familiar with the 1993 US Supreme Court case *South Dakota v. Bourland*. In that case the court reiterated that treaties with aboriginal people and signed by representatives of the United States government are upheld "simply at the *whim* of Congress" (*Tee-Hit-Ton Indians v. U.S.*). In other words, United States Congress can unilaterally nullify a treaty on a *whim*. Congress does not even have to have to supply a reason for abrogating the treaty, something ordinarily needed to justify disregarding an official accord entered into by government representatives. Were this policy of unilateral revocation applied to other treaties, international respect for the U.S. would sharply decline.

In between the two poles of bilateral acceptance (New Zealand) and unilateral revocation (the United States) lies Canada. Here in Canada treaties have some official standing, although not binding recognition as in New Zealand. The Constitution Act of 1982 validates the treaties Canada has signed with First Nations and affirms the land claims established by such compacts. However, the Constitution Act does provide for altering these provisions through a constitutional conference—again, not as extreme as the US position that these can be shifted merely "at the whim of Congress." Furthermore, representatives of First Nations must be invited to attend these conventions. While more generous than the US, these provisions remain less generous than those of New Zealand, where a national tribunal composed of Pakeha and Maori makes binding decisions regarding interpretations of the treaty. Nothing in the Canadian Constitution Act requires that First Nations must approve such changes before they can be enacted into law. Moreover, the prime minister, rather than the Assembly of First Nations, selects leaders invited to the conference (Constitution Act, 1982 Schedule B, Constitution Act, 1982, Part 2 sec. 35). Again, unlike the United States, there remains a role for First Nations, but that role is not as powerful as in New Zealand.

In another respect, Canadian officials differ from their U.S. and New Zealand counterparts. In New Zealand, only a single community, the Maori, inhabited the entire country, necessitating only a single treaty. But in Canada, as in the United States, hundreds of different ethnic and religious communities comprise the Native Americans and First Nations. Many of these groups became part of Canada and the United States without any formal agreements. The Canadian government, unlike the US, has sought to negotiate accords with those First Nations lacking such an arrangement and to enter into written agreements with First Nations on a variety of issues, ranging from self-governance in Manitoba to economic development. The ongoing negotiations leading to signing measures called "written constructive agreements" in various parts of British Columbia signify a willingness to enter into presumably binding negotiated settlements with First Nations. While contemporary New Zealanders have gone the farthest of any former English colony in respecting the bilaterally binding aspects of treaties with natives, and the US in showing disrespect for them in equal measure, Canada, in perhaps typical fashion, falls between the two extremes.

In addition to the political benefits secured by signing treaties, a culturally significant reason also adhered to the process. Colonial governments could and did claim that by physically writing their names on the document, native signatories agreed to the treaty. This claimed consent served to perpetuate the cultural myth of a consensual English takeover of territory. Protests over the absence of real consent have met with differing responses in each of the three treaty nations.

Since 1975, Maori who could prove the lack of consent to earlier land transfers have been allowed compensation in accord with the Treaty of Waitangi (1840). Maori cannot regain ownership of valuable land lost in earlier eras; they must settle for compensation. But they have acquired a right to consent to future losses of territory. Communities have the first refusal (to purchase) when traditional Maori terrain, leased to others, becomes available.

In contrast, the absence of native consent to treaties or land transfers makes no difference to either past or present agreements in the United States. Contemporary refusals to consent to the sale of even marginally valuable land are unapologetically ignored in the United States. For a quarter of a century, the Western Shoshone struggled to hold onto their land—a battle they kept losing, refusing to give up. Their land is western scrub, arid and rough; the brush is prickly and hard to digest, even for most animals: a large stretch of this desert nourishes just a few animals. But despite apparently lacking minerals or anything else of significant economic value, the United States government has steadfastly insisted since the 1970s that the Western Shoshone may not keep their marginal rangeland—despite a treaty allowing them to remain. Two Shoshone sisters repeatedly took their case to the Supreme Court. In its final decision on the matter, the Court stated unequivocally that refusing to consent was not an option the Shoshone Dann sisters had (*United States v. Dann*). Their only option was to accept compensation (at a value a thousand times lower than its lowest fair market value).[4]

In rare circumstances, individual communities in the United States have sometimes managed to regain lost terrain—usually by playing upon the stereotype of the economically unambitious Native American, "the ecological Indian," or the "guardian of sacred sites." Such arguments were successfully employed in 1970 and 1972 when the Nixon administration returned Blue Lake to the Taos and Mount Adams to the Yakama.

In all three nations, native people usually lost ownership of land, the asset most prized by British colonial and subsequent national governments. Furthermore, all three contemporary treaty nations repeatedly deny the possibility of restoring full land ownership to native communities. While the door remains closed to land ownership, no such consensus exists on native ownership of other natural resources.

In New Zealand, Maori and Pakehas (the immigrant-descended New Zealanders)[5] agreed upon shared ownership of fishing rights. While arguing over the meanings of sovereignty and *raratanga*, both sides decided that the treaty clearly excluded the Crown from owning fishing rights. As a result, Maoris have obtained a right to profit from commercial fishing. Today two different types of Maori communities, *iwi* and *hapu*,[6] have what amounts to about a 27% share of the gross profits of Sealord, the major commercial fishing organization in New Zealand (Tribunal, *The Whanganui River Report Wai 167*; Tribunal, *Ngai Tahu Seas Fisheries Report Wai 27*).[7]

While the government of New Zealand remains unique in its willingness to allow Maoris a continuing economic interest in fishing revenues, Canadian and U.S. governments have reacted differently, depending upon a sliding scale of the value of the resources. When oil, the most valuable of all natural resources in the modern world, was discovered in native territories, both the U.S. and Canadian governments sought to terminate those economic interests by a carefully negotiated, agreed upon, one-time payment. The Alaska Native Claims Act in 1971 extinguished the Yupi'k and Inuit claims to aboriginal hunting, fishing, and land rights, and thus cleared the way to the Prudhoe Bay and North Slope oil reserves (*Alaska Native Claims Settlement Act*). In Canada, one quarter of the remaining discovered petroleum and one half of the country's estimated potential petroleum are located north of sixty degrees latitude. In order to obtain ownership of these hydrocarbon-rich parts of otherwise desolate tundra, the Canadian government agreed to create the indigenous province of Nunavut, meaning "our land." Yet Nunavut now controls only seven hundred and seventy thousand square miles of ice and snow. Such carefully scripted accords ensure that natives will be unable to make a future claim upon revenue from these resources.

In the United States the ability to reclaim some small amount of revenue exists with less valuable resources such as timber. In 1974, a previously undiscovered treaty signed by George Washington surfaced in Maine. The treaty granted half of the state to two tribes: the Passamaquoddy and the Penobscot. Shortly after authentication of the treaty, the federal government instantly, and without any explanation, reduced the acreage these two tribes could claim from the treaty-designated twelve and a half to three million acres and excluded from compensation consideration both the populated coast and the valuable timber regions that George Washington had granted them. Instead of twelve and a half (or at the lowest ten) million acres of what had become valuable timberland, the tribes received only three hundred thousand acres of "average quality timberland," plus the option to purchase another two hundred thousand acres of such timberland at their *market* prices (US Comm. on Civil Rights).

In Canada and New Zealand, governments have permitted native communities to retain limited rights over other natural resources because such dominion provides these same administrations with greater political leverage. For example, a handful of corporations control mining and marketing of natural resources, such as copper, zinc, or aluminum. When new finds are uncovered, these corporations usually pressure governments into accepting relatively small payments or royalties. By allowing indigenous communities to retain rights in these regions, governments are able to gain greater leverage over the corporations. In Canada, the government introduces into the negotiations a different arm of the government that claims to represent native people. In Australia and New Zealand, native communities are directly included in negotiations (MacDonald; Stephenson). Only rarely have indigenous communities been able to halt federal initiatives, and then only regarding environmental impact studies (*Taku River Tlingit First Nation v. British Columbia* [Project Assessment Director], [2004] 3 S.C.R. 550, 2004 SCC 74).

Once their negotiating usefulness concludes, however, national or provincial governments customarily secure only a nominal portion of mining revenues for native communities. Later, they fail to exercise reasonable care in seeing that the natives receive what is owed them. In 1998, a conservative federal court judge in the United States found that US government officials, including an internationally famous economist in charge of the US treasury (Robert Rubin), were unable to account for two and a half *billion* dollars in revenues owed Native Americans from oil and gas exploration in Oklahoma (*Cobell v. Kempthorne*).

At the other end of the spectrum, when the resources constitute dangerous contaminants, governments remain largely indifferent. Underneath Native American lands in the United States, for example, are almost all of the United States' uranium supplies. Uranium mining usually causes immense environmental damage, ensuring that the natives will never again be able to use the land for profit. Native communities seeking to become nuclear storage sites have not faced federal opposition.

While British colonial officials often used the formal written agreement to secure indigenous land, in Canada and the United States they sometimes also employed the colonial fiction of native "hunters," that is, "economically unproductive users of the land," to displace aboriginal occupants. While employed piecemeal in Canada and the United States, English colonial officials used this fiction to occupy one entire continent, Australia.

In the eighteenth century, just as British government treaties were beginning to gain purchase, a version of the colonial fiction of native hunters was tried out in Australia. To justify occupation of Australia, the prominent English legal scholar William Blackstone created a new legal fiction called *terra nullius* from a Justinian era law regarding the ownership of hunted animals (*res nullius*) pursued onto another person's property (Blackstone; Seed 155–56, 165). *Nullius* means "of no one," so *terra nullius* means "land of no one"; in other words, there was no one in Australia in 1788, meaning no one capable of owning land.

That legend has been altered (but not entirely eliminated) in the twentieth century. In 1992, the Australian High Court's famous Mabo decision ended the reign of *terra nullius* as officially legitimating English occupation of Australia. In the decision, High Court judges made the surprising observation that in fact Aboriginal people did inhabit Australia prior to the arrival of the English (*Eddi Mabo v. Queensland*, 1992). With *terra nullius* eliminated, another fiction was needed to legitimate the later immigrants' occupation of the territory and to sustain the conviction that Aboriginal communities inherently lacked the right to own land. This new rationale needed to perform the same function as the hunter myth, namely to establish that Aboriginal communities could never have enjoyed legitimate ownership of lands.

The new doctrine created a category of property rights misleadingly termed native, or aboriginal, title. Interestingly enough, this unique device has emerged in all four of the former major English colonies—the three treaty countries, United States, Canada, and New Zealand, as well as Australia. This new regime of property permits natives only contingent use rights. In the United States, Australia, and New Zealand, the arrangement is called "native title" and in Canada "aboriginal title." The US Supreme Court declared that aboriginal interest simply constitutes permission from the whites to occupy the land, and is not specifically recognized as ownership. The Canadian Constitution Act of 1982 similarly defines aboriginal title as the right to exclusive use and occupation of the land, but not ownership. After the celebrated Australian Mabo case (*Mabo v. Queensland*), native title preserved "only an entitlement to use or enjoyment under traditional law or custom" for the Aboriginal people (Australia).

Not all native communities have accepted this new expedient uncritically. In New Zealand, a leading Maori chief explained native title more favourably to his people and more poetically: "The shadow of the land passes to the Queen, but the substance remains with us" (Tribunal, *Muriwhenua Fishing Report* 10.3.3). In all four countries, however, natives are presumed legally to use but not to own land. First Nation claims have usually been transformed from ownership into a request for aboriginal title (*Delgamuukw v. British Columbia*).

But this new legal fiction of mere use rights severely limits the economic potential of native people in two different ways. First, in the Anglo-Saxon legal tradition, land ownership is one key to raising capital. Denying Indians ownership eliminates their ability to use either the land or the valuable assets it contains as collateral for loans for their economic development. Second, lacking legal ownership of the land and its contents, natives cannot sell their land to the highest bidder or take advantage of the market in order to receive a fair price for that land. From Jefferson to Carter, US presidents have fixed an arbitrary figure, considerably less than fair market value, as compensation to natives seeking to sell their lands to the federal government (US Comm. on Civil Rights). Even in New Zealand, the government in 1994 attempted to fix a fiscal or settlement envelope of one billion New Zealand dollars to settle Maori land claims.[8]

When native peoples counter that they will be economically disadvantaged by the inability to sell assets in the open market and at fair market value, opponents frequently charge aboriginal peoples with acting from mere economic motives. The irony never manages to dawn on these usual advocates of capitalism that they are attacking individuals for the right to pursue their own economic self-interest. Behind their incongruously negative attack on self-interest lies an insidious, unstated insistence that only they—non-natives—have the right to pursue profit-making activities. The comment thus marks the desire to retain the colonial fiction—that persistent barrier between natives and latter immigrants—that natives not be allowed to become financial successfully, by using the land, gold, silver, salmon, or even the valuable timber in their terrain. Asserting this thinly veiled ambition to retain economic superiority over indigenous people usually remains unchallenged, making it a classic form of colonial discourse still acceptable today in this seemingly postcolonial world.

A final comparison should emphasize the fact that neither the treaties, nor the colonial fiction of the hunter (not its successor fiction "aboriginal title"), nor the denial of land ownership to indigenous people should be considered inevitable. The contrasts between Anglo colonial attitudes towards native landownership and those in the Iberian world are striking. In Spanish America, popular opinion widely holds that native communities are firmly entitled to own, not merely to use, farmlands and pasturelands, as well other profitable resources, except, of course, for mineral deposits. Several national constitutions and presidential decrees throughout Spanish America in the 1980s and 1990s have reinforced indigenous ownership of traditional lands. The Indigenous Community Statute of Paraguay (1981), the Peruvian Native Communities Act (1974), and the Columbian Constitution of 1991 all recognize indigenous land ownership. The series of ministerial resolutions in Bolivia (1990), the 1994 Constitution, and the land grants by the Ecuadorian government in the 1980s were all passed with widespread public approval. Even the 1987 Philippine Constitution recognizes native ownership and not merely occupation. These principles garner more than official support.

Among the most politically popular aims of the 1993 indigenous uprising in the southern Mexican province of Chiapas (even among urban Mexicans) was the demand that owners of profitable farms return lands to indigenous communities. Leaders of the Chiapas revolt demanded that all poor quality land in excess of a hundred hectares and all good quality land in excess of fifty hectares be taken away from landowners, who would remain as smallholders or join the cooperative farmers' movement, farming societies, or communal land (Marcos).

Yet such moves are decidedly unpopular in the United States. The Maine Congressional Delegation on February 28, 1977 states, "There is no equitable way of forcing a return to [to natives of] land which has been settled, developed and improved in good faith by Maine people for two centuries" (Rights 130). The same argument, raised by hacendados in Chiapas who claimed to have the right to retain "settled, developed and improved" land, confronted political and cultural opposition; mere economic profit-making did not constitute an acceptable reason for refusing to return indigenous land that had been illegally acquired.

In Ibero-America, when documentation of a native claim to land is discovered, the burden of proof lies with the non-Indian owner. Current owners must prove that they and other non-Indians acquired the land legitimately. Some national governments are even committed to helping natives recover written or pictorial evidence of old titles. The National Archives of Mexico, for example, has a full-time staff fluent in native languages available to help Native Americans who have come to find and identify documentary evidence of land that they owned as recently as twenty years ago or as long ago as the sixteenth century. While the original Spanish Covenant with the subjugated communities guaranteeing such ownership applied only to agricultural communities, the tradition has created a contemporary presumption in favour of such rights, even in regions of mixed nomadic and sedentary peoples. Thus, formerly nomadic communities on the periphery of Mexico, Chile, and Ecuador can rely upon a tradition that favours native communities retaining their traditional lands. Relying upon that tradition allowed nomadic Mapuche to obtain more than a hundred and eighty-five thousand acres in a recent settlement from the government of Chile, and a still larger amount from the government of Argentina. Both governments actually returned land ownership to Indian communities.

The willingness of postcolonial Hispanic societies to allow indigenous land ownership, however, does not extend to identical rights over their labour. As a result, concern over labour abuses dominates historical studies and contemporary scholarship on indigenous people in Ibero-America. Just the opposite is true in Anglo North America. Alice Littlefield and Martha C. Knack write, "Studies of North American Indian economic life have largely ignored the participation of indigenous people in wage labour, even though for over a century such participation has been essential for the survival of native individuals and communities" (Littlefield and Knack 3). The central topic in scholarship in the three treaty nations remains land.

Throughout the Americas, nationalists often assert that their colonial or present-day treatment of natives is superior to others. Not only are they vying for the dubious honour of proving the advantages of one colonial project over another, they are also unquestioningly assuming the validity of their own judgements about the proper path to riches. For the belief that certain goods belong to others, while others can be appropriated, rests on nothing more solid than historically and culturally constructed judgements about economics. The belief that colonists can occupy native land lacks merit, just as does the conviction that colonists have a right to their labour.

But until citizens of former English and Iberian colonies understand that national traditions follow colonial ones, there will be no possibility of overcoming the still colonial position of native peoples within the nations of the Americas. Decolonization of the Americas and other lands requires that we no longer see each other as distorted reflections of each other, but as fellow humans on the planet. For indigenous peoples of the Americas, New Zealand, and Australia, there was and still is no perfect world.

1 When referring to native communities generically, this piece employs the lower case. When referring to a specific community, such as Native Americans, the upper case appears.

2 An exception is Roger Maaka and Augie Fleras, *The Politics of Indigeneity: Challenging The State in Canada and Aotearoa, New Zealand* (Dunedin, N.Z.: University of Otago Press, 2005).

3 The words are *tratar* (Spanish and Portuguese), *traiter* (French), and *trakteren* (Dutch). Another commonly used word in Dutch, *verdrag*, came from the word meaning to endure or tolerate.

4 On the open market, the 27 million acres were worth between $250 and $1,000 an acre, making the entire area worth $144 billion dollars. The Indian Claims Commission offered $140 million. The effort to move the Shoshone off the land became more urgent when low grade gold ore was discovered in the 1990s near the Dann sisters' land.

5 A characteristic difference between European colonial settlements in Polynesia and in the Americas lies in the pattern of mutual naming. Unlike the Americas where Europeans initially named natives "Indians," throughout Polynesia immigrant communities adopted indigenous people's names for themselves. Thus the nineteenth- and twentieth century immigrant New Zealanders soon adopted the Maori term for non-Maori settlers, *Pakeha*. Similar processes occurred throughout the Polynesian areas—Tonga, Vanuatu, and Samoa, where variants of "papalangi" emerged. Since the 1990s, however, increasingly greater numbers of people have identified themselves as simply "New Zealand" or "New Zealanders."

6 The distinction is under dispute—and does not easily fit into territorial, kinship, or descent categories. The Te Ture Whenua Maori Act of 1993 considers *hapu* to comprise groups of families sharing a common ancestor, and *iwi* territorial/ ancestral combinations of *hapu*. Complications exist because in the 2000 census, nearly a third of all Maori did not (or refused to) identify themselves as members of any *iwi*, and territorial boundaries of *iwi* often completely overlap (http://www.stats.govt.nz/products-and-services/Articles/changes-ethnicity-2001-cens-pop-dwell.htm). A significant percentage of Maori identify themselves as members of more than one *iwi*.

7 These are my estimates, because New Zealand divides up fishing quotas by species, and the percentage of Maori profits varies according to the species. The calculations are complicated, but it winds up at about a 27% share of the profits.

8 New Zealand cancelled the overall fiscal envelope policy in 1996, following Maori protest. However, the government has since pursued the fiscal envelope strategy on an *iwi* by *iwi* basis. "Consideration of Reports Submitted by States Parties under Article 9 of the Convention," *Committee on the Elimination of Racial Discrimination*, 61st ed. (New York: M. Nijhoff, 2002).

THREE

"THE RIGHTS TO THE LAND MAY BE TRANSFERRED"

Archival Records as Colonial Text—A Narrative of Métis Scrip

Frank Tough & Erin McGregor

Introduction: Problem, Place, and Period

IN 1994, THE MÉTIS of Northwest Saskatchewan launched a land claim against the governments of Canada and Saskatchewan.[1] To satisfy this claim they must meet three basic challenges: first, the Métis must demonstrate their existence as an Aboriginal people;[2] second, they must show their historic and contemporary land use and occupancy patterns in Northwest Saskatchewan, thereby establishing a proprietary claim to Aboriginal title;[3] and third, the Métis must prove that their Aboriginal title existed at the time of effective Canadian sovereignty. Similarly, any valid claims to Aboriginal rights must be based on the identification of specific activities that were practised at the time of Canadian control. Specifically, the Métis need to address the effect of the government's "Half-breed" scrip policies on their propriety interests in order to counter the government's legal claim that their Aboriginal title was clearly and plainly extinguished.

Our study here contributes to this third challenge by first establishing a general model of the land scrip system, and then examining one individual scrip claimant's paper trail in order to illustrate the ways in which this system might have failed to meet the standards of existing conventions for conveying interests in property. As arcane as the history of Métis scrip is, an understanding of the details of colonial land systems that became a central foundation of the Canadian nation state is necessary to work out the sharing of space today between Indigenous peoples and the present-day descendents of settler society.[4]

Abundant historical records exist to demonstrate the distinctive qualities of the Métis society that emerged in what is now Northwest Saskatchewan, along with accounts of their use of lands and resources.

The Métis refer to themselves as *Otipimsuak*, a Cree word meaning "the free people" or, literally, "people who own themselves." Although far removed from the power centres of contemporary urban Canada, a fascinating history and geography shaped the development of this Aboriginal society in Northwest Saskatchewan. This region, referred to as the English River District by the management of the Hudson's Bay Company (HBC), was a contact zone for the Dene and Cree peoples who were essential for the prosperity of the fur trade and crucial to the formation of Métis communities. This northern region was well suited to the many demands of the fur trade. The Métis, progeny of the intermarriage between European traders and Indigenous women, made the fur trade their occupation and this region their home.

A major continental divide or "height of land" separates the drainage systems of the Mackenzie/Athabasca from the Churchill/Hudson Bay rivers. By 1776, Montreal trading interests had penetrated the Athabasca country. The crossing of this drainage divide over the Methy Portage is a little known but truly monumental event in Canadian nation building. Thereafter, the development of the Methy Portage tied the rich fur country of the Athabasca and Mackenzie regions to the commercial expansion of the society of the St. Lawrence valley and, to a lesser degree in the competitive era (but much more so after 1821), to the rival interests of the HBC, which shipped fur to London through York Factory. The English River District posts along the Green Lake/Portage La Loche corridor served as a vital nexus in the Canadian fur trade, providing access to more northerly trade routes and creating a strong demand for the skills and talents of the Métis (e.g. trading, interpreting, provisioning, guiding, and transporting). The strategic importance of this region was reflected in the intense, and at times violent, local competition between Montreal and English merchants. Because of this rivalry, an HBC post was not permanently established at Île-à-la-Crosse until 1814. The posts at Île-à-la-Crosse, Green Lake, and Portage La Loche were the forerunners of today's Métis communities.

As a result of the creation of a commercial monopoly in 1821, the HBC assumed certain obligations towards Aboriginal people and, concomitantly, Métis communities continued to provide labour and products for the HBC. After 1870, when the Dominion of Canada acquired the HBC territory,[5] the perseverance of a fur industry in Northwest Saskatchewan provided stability for Métis communities of the English River District. Because fur trade resource needs required an extensive land base, the annual cycle of Aboriginal economic activities involved living off the land and periodic visits to posts. By the mid-nineteenth century, the concentration of French/Michif-speaking Métis people was so significant that Île-à-la-Crosse was selected as the site of the first Oblate mission outside of the Red River Settlement. A permanent mission, housing a contingent of French-speaking priests and nuns, became a part of the community.[6]

According to census and treaty records, the Métis at the turn of the twentieth century constituted the largest part of the Aboriginal population of Northwest Saskatchewan.[7] An analysis of Métis scrip applications indicates a high degree of population stability, making the situation here markedly different from the out-migration experienced by the Red River Métis after 1870.[8] The demographic significance of the Métis in Northwest Saskatchewan did not diminish. A 1971 population survey established that there were 4,395 Métis living in Northwest Saskatchewan and only 1,200 Indians.[9] From a broader geographical and historical perspective, this region is a highly significant regional homeland for the Métis Nation. Clearly, the Métis of Northwest Saskatchewan, unlike the Métis of the Red River Settlement, did not relocate or disperse en masse, nor were they subsumed by newcomers. The history and demography of this region exhibit a strong, continuing Métis presence.

The transition between HBC/mission dominance and the establishment of state agencies occurred incrementally after 1870. Through Treaty Ten in 1906, the federal government established Canada's formal presence in the region. The enforcement of conservation regulations was also an important impetus for state formation in northern Saskatchewan. Shortly after the onset of provincial control over natural resources in 1930, federal and provincial efforts were made to support the Native economy. Following the 1944 provincial election of a social democratic government, a system of extensive fur conservation blocks was organized with the intention that communities could sustain themselves through hunting, trapping, and commercial fishing. Once well suited to the specialized needs of the fur trade, and despite the growth of uranium mining, forestry, and tourism, this region continues to sustain a traditional economy based on trapping, hunting, and fishing.

Due to the long history of trade in Northwest Saskatchewan, the roots of Métis society in the region run deep. The Métis people of this region trace their ancestry to the French-Canadian and a few Anglo-Celtic employees of fur trading companies who came to the region in the late eighteenth and early nineteenth centuries, and to the Cree and Dene peoples indigenous to the area. This region, once a vital link in an expansive mercantile economic system that served as the geographic foundation of the Canadian nation state, is today largely a forgotten space, as are the Métis who have made this region their homeland for generations.[10]

With respect to the land claim, we are confident that the archival records will establish the nature of the Métis society that developed in Northwest Saskatchewan.[11]

In 1999, the University of Alberta was contracted to conduct archival research related to this claim, filed in 1994, on behalf of the Métis Nation–Saskatchewan. The research team, based at the School of Native Studies, set out to identify, locate, obtain, and compile archival records relating to the fundamental challenges of establishing a factual and valid claim. From the start it was decided to digitize these records, and much effort has been directed towards the conversion of archival information into searchable text stored in the form of databases. To a lesser extent than desired, efforts have been directed towards the scanning of maps, photographs, and documents. Early on, the research team adopted the moniker "matriX" (Metis Aboriginal Title Research Initiative–X) which reflects our unapologetic efforts to develop as precise a Cartesian-like control over the seeming chaos of a vast, complex documentary record deriving from a variety of repositories. Our method is indicative of a commitment to deal seriously with the contrasting "realities" of the scrip system.[12] Over the past several years, the matriX Project has employed students, generally undergraduates, to conduct research and to database archival records. By scrutinizing archival documents and reconstructing paper trails, our work provides important insights into how the scrip system was implemented. While the research is still in progress, we have developed a comprehensive appreciation for the Métis scrip system as a rather obscure feature of Canada's historical consciousness. Further, by transcribing the archival documents in a systematic and organized way, we have begun to unveil the layered complexities of the relationship between colonial policy, Métis communities, and the economic dynamics of the emerging Canadian nation.

Scrip Coupons: Paper or Land?

"Scrip" is a term used to denote "a certificate, voucher, etc. establishing the bearer's right to something" ("Scrip"). According to government officials then and now, Métis scrip, officially known as "Halfbreed" scrip, was issued to Métis people with the intent of "extinguishing" Indian title by granting land (or money) to individual Métis people. Figure 1 is a digital reproduction of a land coupon, redeemable for 80 acres of Dominion lands, drawn up in favor of Eli Roy on 2 October 1907. Figure 2 depicts his other coupon, in the amount of 160 acres. The scrip process entailed more than government officials simply issuing coupons printed on high quality banknote paper. Because the individual interest in a scrip

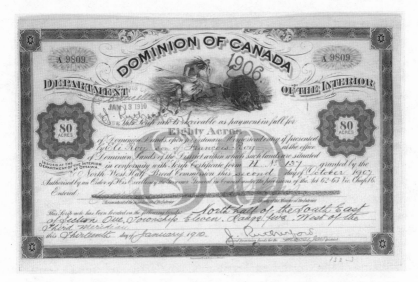

FIGURE 1   Land Scrip Coupon (A9809) for 80 acres issued to Eli Roy, son of Francois Roy, located on N 1/2 of SE 1/4 of Section 1, Township 11, Range 5, West of the Third Meridian on 13 January 1910 at Moose Jaw.

FIGURE 2   Land Scrip Coupon (A8770) for 160 acres issued to Eli Roy, son of Francois Roy, located on SE 1/4 of Section 13, Township 32, Range 26, West of the Second Meridian on 25 November 1919 at Humboldt.

Frank Tough & Erin McGregor   37

THOMPSON-NICOLA REGIONAL DISTRICT LIBRARY SYSTEM

coupon could be converted to real interests in land, an elaborate system evolved to determine who was entitled to the coupons and how these coupons could be disposed of in ways that would meet the needs of scrip buyers. Put simply, paper could be converted into land. In a crude way, scrip might be regarded as compensation for surrendering proprietary interests in what we know today as "Aboriginal title." Or perhaps scrip is another example of the humane and just treatment of Indigenous people by the rule of Anglo-Canadian law. In any case, scrip coupons increasingly came to symbolize the historical relationship between Métis people and the Government of Canada. To the extent that modern land claims are a mutual effort to rectify past injustices, an understanding of how the scrip system was implemented will contribute to the narrative of Métis land claims.[13]

The Government of Canada offered two types of coupons to Métis claimants of the Northwest Territories: land scrip and money scrip.[14] Land scrip could be exchanged by the grantee at par for acres of Dominion lands, that is, lands ordinarily open for homesteading in the prairie provinces.[15] Land scrip was usually doled out as two separate coupons in units of eighty acres and one hundred and sixty acres (see Figures 1 and 2).[16] Money scrip was issued in dollar units and could be converted by the bearer into Dominion lands; however, the acreage of land that could be obtained with a money scrip coupon depended upon prices set by the Interior Department. Early in the settlement of the prairie west, Dominion lands often sold for a dollar an acre. As land values increased over time, 160 dollars of money scrip would not buy 160 acres of homestead lands.[17] Since Dominion lands could be purchased with cash, it appears that money scrip was destined to be discounted from its face value, otherwise money scrip held no advantage for a buyer over a straight cash purchase of Dominion lands.[18] With the rapid settlement of the prairies after 1897 and the increase in the price of Dominion homestead lands, land scrip gained real value over money scrip. Consequently, after 1900, the amount of land scrip selected by claimants increased significantly relative to money scrip.[19] In the first decade of the twentieth century, land scrip became an important mechanism to obtain homestead lands.

A crucial difference between these two types of scrip was ease of convertibility. Land scrip was used to initiate a "chain of title" that necessitated many records, creating a large, complicated, and in some cases convoluted, paper trail.[20] While the name of the grantee appeared on the face of land scrip and the grantee had personally to select a plot of land, money scrip was more easily converted into land because the name of the grantee did

THOMPSON-NICOLA REGIONAL DISTRICT LIBRARY SYSTEM

not in most cases appear on the face of the coupon and it could be redeemed at any Dominion Land Office by whoever bore the coupon.

The Land Scrip Process: A General Model

The scrip system raises fundamental questions about Métis Aboriginal title and about the way scrip coupons were used in the transformation of prairie land use and tenure. The implementation of this system under Anglo-colonial politics and law was intricate and perplexing on many levels. To date, we have not found a government document that explains the entire process of Métis scrip, so we have reconstructed the manner in which government officials understood and implemented the process (see Figure 3). This model represents the government's view of the formal procedures and projected outcomes, and it might well be regarded as how the scrip system was supposed to work.[21] The land scrip system characterized in Figure 3 is representative of the claims taken by the 1906 Treaty Ten scrip commission, but also holds generally for other scrip commissions.[22]

Under authority of the Dominion Lands Act, the process began when the Privy Council (in effect, the cabinet) passed one or more Orders-in-Council, appointing a scrip commissioner and providing criteria to determine who qualified for scrip (Phase 1).[23] Between 1885 and 1925 a number of distinct scrip commissions were created to deal with Métis in the North West Territories (Tough, "Activities of Metis Scrip Commissions," 61–62). Scrip commissioners would then visit communities to take claims and issue certificates to bona fide claimants. A Métis claimant would complete a declaration (or application) in the presence of the commissioner, and this declaration would be supported by a witness declaration, with information usually provided by an individual familiar with the claimant (Phase 2). Since many claimants would be known to local Hudson's Bay Company officials and missionaries, these additional sources of personal information provided assistance to commissioners in validating an individual's claim. The application would then be reviewed by the commissioner and staff, checked against ledger books that listed previous claimants, and, if the claimant met specific criteria, the claim would be approved. If the claimant did not meet the specific criteria, the claim would be rejected, but in certain instances a claim with potential might be reserved.[24] A Certificate of Entitlement, signed by the commissioner, confirmed that the claimant was entitled to scrip. One copy of this certificate was retained by the Department of the Interior and the other went to the Métis grantee. This certificate indicated approval of the claim and seems to have had market value, but was not the actual coupon.[25] Following the work of the commission, documentation was sent to Ottawa and maintained by the Land Patents Branch of the Department of the Interior. Large ledger books tracked the details of each claim, the delivery of coupons, and the conversion of land scrip to Dominion lands.

The grantee would then send the certificate of entitlement to the Department of the Interior in Ottawa in order to have the certificate exchanged for scrip coupons (Phase 4). An "issue order" directed the Department's accountant to issue coupons, thereby confirming the entitlement promised by the certificate. Scrip coupons were printed on quality paper, resembled bonds, and had serial numbers (see Figures 1 and 2). These serial numbers have enabled us to reconstruct the scrip system, and serve as a key to tracking individual claims because the connections between documents can be established by these serial numbers. In Phase 4, the scrip coupons were delivered to the grantee (the "Agent/Present Owner," in the language of the delivery register), and delivery was acknowledged by the recipient, who signed a receipt that was returned to the Interior Department in Ottawa. At this point, the grantee held the required documentation to convert the coupon, a piece of paper, into a tangible piece of real property.

The conversion of the piece of paper into land began with the locating of the scrip coupon. The "locating" of the coupon entailed a registration of the grantee's interest in a precisely-defined parcel of land that had been acquired or secured by the entitlement promised by the coupon (Phase 4). Applying the coupons to a parcel of land represented another phase of the paper trail, which ultimately would have resulted in the grantee obtaining fee simple title to a total of 240 acres of land. Procedures and rules governed the conversion of the coupons into a land patent. Land scrip coupons could only be applied to lands ordinarily open to homestead entry. (Thus Métis scrip could not be used to secure title to homestead lands that had already been selected and occupied by a homesteader, and it could not be used to obtain land in the regions that had not been surveyed into townships.) At a Dominion Lands Office, the Métis grantee would present the scrip coupons to a Dominion Lands Agent and select 160 and 80 acres of land from those lands open for homesteading.[26] The location was then "entered" or the coupon "located." In effect, the grantee's interest in a particular parcel of land was registered. Local Dominion Lands offices kept track of the locales of specific tenures and lands available for settlement for the land districts under their jurisdiction.

A necessary procedure known as the "Rule of Location" required the grantee, and not any other individual, to locate the coupon. According to a Department of the Interior bulletin of 2 January 1930,

Phase 1: *Establishment* (OTTAWA)

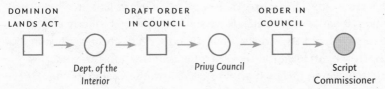

Phase 2: *Application* (IN COUNTRY)

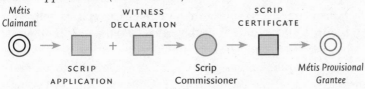

Phase 3: *Paper Entitlement* (OTTAWA / IN COUNTRY)

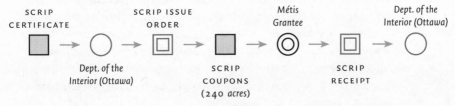

Phase 4: *Location* (DOMINION LANDS OFFICE)

Phase 5: *Patent* (OTTAWA)

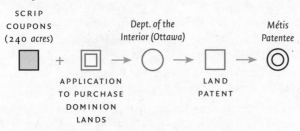

FIGURE 3   Land Scrip—The General Model, *ca.* 1907.

Land scrip cannot be assigned. Entry for land upon which it is desired to apply the scrip can only be made by the half-breed to whom it has been issued.... No assignment of right to scrip is recognized, but after the half-breed land scrip has been applied to land, *the rights to the land may be transferred.* No transfer of such right, however, executed prior to the date of the location of the scrip on the land or executed by a person under twenty-one years of age may be recognized.[27]

In effect, there are several rules or requirements associated with locating land scrip: (1) the grantee must be present; (2) the right or interests cannot be assigned to another party until the coupon has been located/registered; and (3) the grantee must be an adult in order to assign or transfer the right or interest in the land. Under the Rule of Location, the Métis grantee initiates a chain of title in a government land office by selecting a parcel of land with the acreage corresponding to the entitlement provided on the face of the coupon. The land could then only be assigned or transferred to another party by an adult after the specific land interest had been established and registered. Significantly, the assignment/transfer/conveyance of the grantee's interest to another party could occur before Ottawa officials issued a patent to the land. In such instances, the patent was issued in the name of the party (assignee) who received the assignment.

Most prairie lands were "untitled" before 1870, and it was through the Dominion Land system that "good titles" were created.[28] The granting of good title by the Crown, along with a system for the registration of titles, was an orderly approach to settlement. Within the framework of Anglo-Canadian colonial property law, the orderly development of vast unsettled and untitled lands required the establishment of a process for granting good titles. The Rule of Location appears to have been an attempt to keep the records straight by providing a legal basis for title, thereby permitting and facilitating subsequent conveyances of land, although, from the perspective of today's cultural fundamentalists, it might seem like an annoying and alien imposition on Métis communities. No doubt, some will entertain the notion that the unrestricted market and private conveyancing would have been a better approach to Métis interests.[29]

The scrip coupons and application for location (legally defined parcel of land) were sent to the Land Patents Branch in Ottawa (Phase 5). This documentation would then be processed in the same manner as other applications for patents to Dominion lands, such as the conversion of the right of occupancy by a homestead tenure to a fee simple title. If there were no complications concerning title, the Métis grantee would receive a Letter Patent for the located land and the patentee's fee simple ownership would be registered in the local Land Titles office, a procedure consistent with the registration of individual property interests. The Letter Patent declared the grantee's right "To have and to hold unto the grantee in fee simple" the land to which s/he was entitled.[30] Such elaborate procedures concerning Métis land scrip were consistent with the registration of individual property interests in the land system that the Interior Department had created in the prairies after 1870. Large ledgers were kept to register the details of the location of land scrip, the assignment of grantee interests, and the particulars of letters patent. While an understanding of the "official" model of the land scrip system provides some conceptual clarity, this model needs to be considered and evaluated against actual experience.

Eli Roy's Experience with Land Scrip

The above "official" model of the scrip process also enables us to analyze the vast documentation generated by many transactions involving thousands of Métis grantees. In order to determine how this intricate process was specifically implemented, we developed databases and spreadsheets to capture and organize archival materials. This technique permits an orderly and disciplined examination of many documents and the connections between them. Our research approach is facilitated by the fact that standardized forms were used and key documents (applications, certificates, and coupons) were given serial numbers by Interior Department officials. Initial findings indicate a much more complex and multi-dimensional process at work than that generally offered in the scholarly literature on the subject.[31] Indeed, our research suggests a narrative of the scrip system and those involved in it that departs widely from the official model. The following case study of a Métis man, Eli Roy, provides an alternative to the official government narrative of Métis scrip. Indeed, Roy's case foregrounds irregularities and incongruities that seem to typify the way in which the scrip system was implemented in the early twentieth century.

Privy Council Order No. 1459 on 20 July 1906 established the commission that treated with Indians and issued scrip to the Métis of northern Saskatchewan.[32] Roy's two-page scrip application declaration (Form A) is reproduced as Figure 4. Eli Roy's verbal answers to the questions would have been recorded on this document by the commissioner or more likely by his clerk. Roy's declaration was supported by a witness declaration, provided by Roy's godfather Thomas Desjarlais (Form A-2, Figure 5).[33]

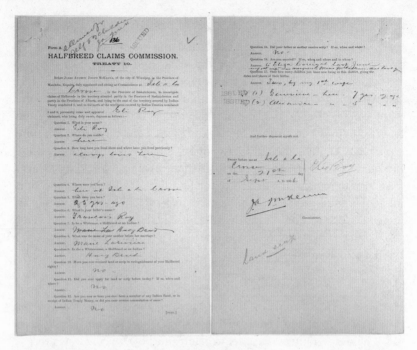

FIGURE 4   Eli Roy's Application for Scrip (Form A) [2 pages].

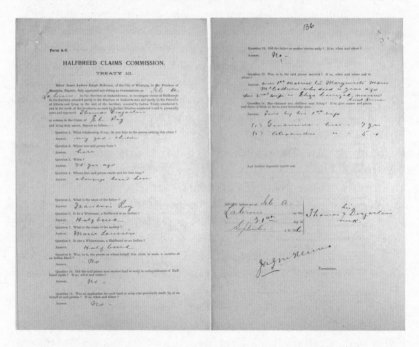

FIGURE 5   Witness Declaration (Form A 2) supporting Eli Roy's Scrip Claim [2 pages].

"The Rights to the Land May Be Transferred"

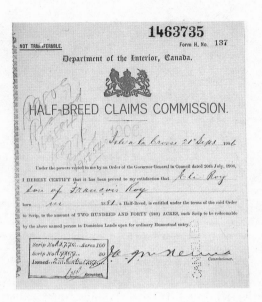

FIGURE 6   Scrip Certificate (Form H) issued by the 1906 Half-breed Claims Commission to Eli Roy, son of Francois Roy, on 21 September 1906 [copy from file 1463735].

Roy's scrip claim was approved and his certificate (Form H, No. 137) was issued on the date of application, 21 September 1906 (Figure 6).[34] Commissioner J.A.J. McKenna certified that Roy was a Half-breed entitled to "Scrip to the amount of TWO HUNDRED AND FORTY (240) ACRES," which could be redeemed "by the above named person in Dominion Lands open for ordinary Homestead entry."[35] Charles Mair, commissioner secretary, witnessed Roy's receipt of the certificate.

On 27 September 1907, G.D. Boulton, Manager of the Imperial Bank of Canada (Ottawa Branch), forwarded four certificates, including Form H, No. 137, which had been issued to Eli Roy, to the secretary of the Department of the Interior, P.D. Keyes, requesting an exchange of the enclosed certificates for the grantees' coupons.[36] On the same day, the Chief Clerk W. S. Giddon drew up a scrip issue order that was approved by W.W. Cory, Deputy Minister of the Interior (Figure 7). The preparation of the actual coupons did not take long. On 2 October 1907, scrip coupons A8770 (160 Acres) and A9809 (80 acres) were issued (see Figures 1 and 2). The next day, Keyes forwarded eight scrip coupons, including those granted to Eli Roy, to the Imperial Bank of Canada in Ottawa.[37] Evidently, his coupons were then sent to a Winnipeg Branch of the Imperial Bank of Canada, since the assistant manager of that branch signed Eli Roy's receipt (Form No. 65) on 12 October and this receipt was received by the Department of the Interior on 16 October (Figure 8). Again this paper-

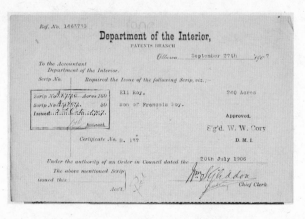

FIGURE 7   Scrip Coupon Issue Order for Eli Roy on 27 September 1907 [copy from file 1463735].

work passed though the Ottawa Branch of the Imperial Bank of Canada before arriving at the Department of the Interior on 16 October 1907.[38]

A little more than a year after Roy's claim had been recognized by a certificate issued by Treaty Ten and Scrip Commissioner McKenna at Ilê-à-la-Crosse, his certificate was exchanged for land scrip coupons (A8770 and A9809). Significantly, the grantee did not initiate the exchange of his certificate for coupons. How his and many other Métis individuals' certificates came into the possession of the Ottawa Branch of the Imperial Bank is unknown at this point. Apparently, no documentation confirming lawful possession of the certificate by the bank was required in order for the Department of the Interior to issue coupons in exchange for Roy's certificate. Those interested in obtaining coupons (i.e. scrip buyers) travelled with scrip commissions and purchased certificates at the time of issue. Proof of receipt of the actual coupons did not have to be provided by the Métis grantee; the delivery ledger books accommodated this discrepancy by simply referring to the coupon recipient under the heading of "Agent/ Present Owner."[39] Not infrequently, scrip coupons were delivered to banks. In the case of the delivery register information for Roy, the delivery details and receipt number are missing. Correspondence between bank managers and Interior officials and the actual receipt document provides vital details about the process. In early October 1907, the Winnipeg Branch of the Imperial Bank of Canada was in possession of Eli Roy's coupons. Although Interior officials often claimed that "no assignment of right to scrip is recognized," third parties, and not the Métis grantees, were in almost every case in possession of the land scrip coupons.

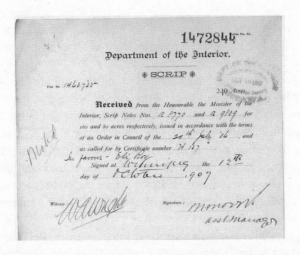

FIGURE 8   Receipt (Form 65) for Scrip Coupons A8770 and A9809 signed at Winnipeg 12 October 1907 [copy from file 1463735].

After the coupons had been delivered to a bank, several years passed before Roy's coupons were converted to actual grants of land. The face of the scrip coupons provides evidence about the redemption of the grant. Roy's 160-acre scrip coupon was redeemed at the Humbolt Dominion Land Office on 25 November 1909 and located on SE 1/4 section 13, township 32, range 26 west of the second meridian, on 158.70 acres (see Figure 2). Alex L'Esperance witnessed Roy's application for the land.[40] His coupon for 80 acres was redeemed at the Moose Jaw Dominion Land Office on 13 January 1910, and located on northern half of SE 1/4 section 1, township 11, range 5, west of the third meridian on 81 acres (Figure 1).[41] Hence, Roy's interest in two particular, legally described parcels of land was established and registered at two different land offices.

If compliance with the Rule of Location occurred, Eli Roy would have had to have made two trips to southern Dominion Land Offices in order to deal with his two land scrip coupons. The first trip, in 1909 to Humbolt, Saskatchewan, entailed a straight-line distance of 410 kms or 543 kms by today's road network. The second trip, in early January 1910, is 590 kms straight distance, or 701 kms by today's roads, to Moose Jaw. To locate the coupons in Humboldt and Moose Jaw and return to Ilê-à-la-Crosse, Roy would have traveled between 2000 and 2582 kms. Since Eli Roy did not personally acquire title to these lands through a Letter Patent from the Lands Patent Branch of the Department of the Interior, it is not clear what would have motivated him or other northern Métis grantees to travel to distant land offices. If Roy engaged in hunting, trapping, and fishing, these trips would have taken him away from the trapping grounds during harvest time.

The Location Registers, maintained by the Department of the Interior, recorded core details about the conveyance of Métis grantee interests in the homestead lands located and about the issuing of Letters Patent. Homestead files created by the Department of the Interior, now in the custody of the prairie provincial archives, are also important documentary sources concerning the conversion of coupons into land titles (see Figures 9 and 10). And since Eli Roy's scrip coupons recorded a legal description of the lands located, his interests developed the appearance of real property. The 158.70-acre parcel was assigned to Laurence A. Walch of Winnipeg. On 21 December 1909, at Ilê-à-la-Crosse, Roy transferred his interests to Walch by signing a Quit Claim Deed, witnessed by Arthur H. Pierce and Angus McKay, for the sum, according to this document, of $700. On 25 February 1910, Walch forwarded the deed purportedly executed by Eli Roy to the Department of the Interior.[42] Assignment No. 17378 was registered on 16 March 1910 and verified by N.O. Cote (Figure 9). A Dominion patent for 158.70 acres was issued to Walch on 22 March 1910.[43]

Roy's other coupon was redeemed on 13 January 1910.[44] This 81-acre parcel was assigned to Emile Gravel, a farmer, on 14 January 1910. The assignment was conveyed in Moose Jaw the day after Eli Roy is purported to have located the land. On 4 February 1910, Cote registered Assignment No. 17323 (see Figure 10). A Dominion patent for these 81 acres was issued to Emile Gravel on 4 February 1910.[45] While the records generated by the scrip system document very specific property interests, they do not tell us how the scrip coupons journeyed from the Winnipeg Branch of the Imperial Bank to Dominion Lands Offices in Humboldt and Moose Jaw.

In the official model of the land scrip system, once land had been located and the scrip coupon redeemed, the Métis grantee could then either have filed for a Letter Patent (equivalent to today's Certificate of Title) or "sold" his/her interest in land acquired by redemption of their coupons. Clearly, this is not what happened in Eli Roy's case. Because Eli Roy did not take possession of the coupons or obtain a Letter Patent, his experience deviates significantly from the official model. His case is not unique: of 742 land scrip coupons issued in the Claim Region, 725 were assigned to third parties, and only 3 coupons were converted by the grantee to a Letter Patent.[46]

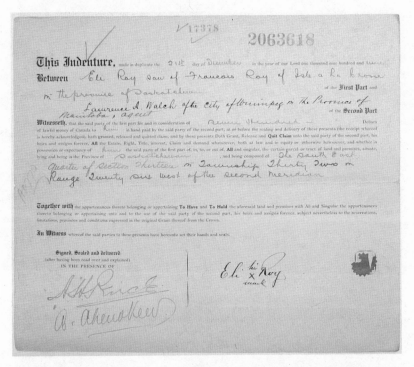

FIGURE 9   Assignment No. 17378 transferring Eli Roy's interests in SE 1/4 of Section 13, Township 32, Range 26, West of the Second Meridian to Laurence A. Walch on 21 December 1909 in Ilê-à-la-Crosse [2 pages].

X Marks The Spot

Rather than dismissing these records as culturally insensitive artifacts of Eurocentrism, we have been interrogating them in order to determine how the scrip system worked. Unless the manner in which this system was implemented is known in detail, it is not possible to determine what specific outcomes resulted and whether or not these outcomes were equitable for the Métis communities involved. An accurate representation of the scrip system will also illuminate the relationship between Métis communities and the Crown. Because the collective Métis interests in their Aboriginal title were magically transformed (in the view of the government officials of the era) into some rather vague or potential but conveniently alienable interests in individual fee simple titles, the propriety of that particular property system needs initially to be considered on its own terms as a foundation for further analysis. Most clearly, compliance with the Rule of Location and the validity of the transfer of the grantee's land interest to third parties are the fundamental property issues.[47] Once

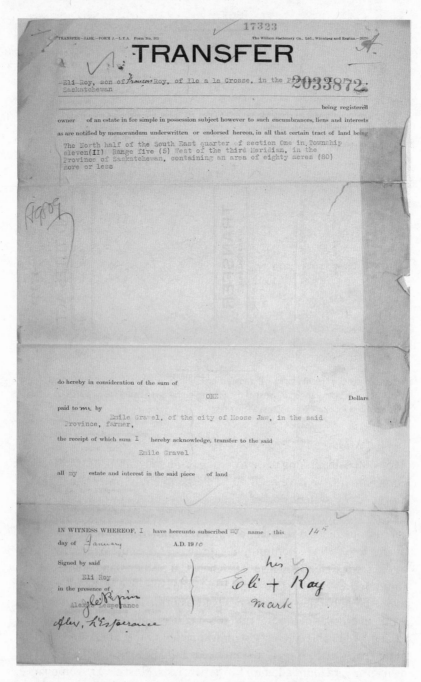

FIGURE 10 Assignment No. 17323 transferring Eli Roy's interests in N 1/2 of S E 1/4 of Section 1, Township 11, Range 5, West of the Third Meridian to Emile Gravel on 14 January 1910 in Moose Jaw [2 pages].

50 *"The Rights to the Land May Be Transferred"*

these details are analyzed, we will have a better understanding of the extent to which the Crown fulfilled its obligation to deal honourably with Aboriginal peoples and interests (including lands).

As an initial appraisal, three empirical tests can be employed to consider the validity of the land scrip system: (1) the physical possession of scrip coupons; (2) the consistency of signature representations on documents; and (3) the geographical proximity between the home communities of grantees and the locales where coupons were located and land interests were assigned. The inability to prove credible on any one of these criteria is problematic, but a failure to appear credible on two or all three tests poses a serious challenge to the very validity of the scrip system. If serious doubts exist about the participation of grantees in locating and conveying land scrip interests, and/or if those in possession of the coupons (such as the agent or present owner) also had motives to circumvent the Rule of Location, then the scrip system was implemented in a manner that was inconsistent with the property conventions of the day that upheld standards for registering and transferring ownership. Furthermore, if the scrip system, as a facet of the emerging colonial land tenure order, failed on its own peculiar terms, then fundamental questions must ensue about the merits of this system to satisfy any long-term Aboriginal interests of the Métis arising out of their interactions with the European settlement frontier.[48]

Eli Roy's scrip coupons were not delivered to him but to a bank in Winnipeg, following a request made through the Ottawa Branch of the same bank. Our analysis indicates that of the 1015 coupon delivery destinations associated with the Claim Region, only 17 or 1.7 percent of the grantees received their coupons in person, while the rest were delivered to third parties or to the grantee in care of a third party. Of 1015 grants, 336 were delivered to banks and 173 to law firms.[49] Some 991 coupons were delivered outside of the study region.[50] The delivery of Eli Roy's coupons to a third party, a bank, was not exceptional. Grantees did not physically possess their coupons; the Department of the Interior established a delivery system that allowed third parties to take possession of both money and land scrip coupons.[51]

Several documents (Figures 4, 9, and 10) indicate inconsistent signatures and marks. A few years before McKenna's scrip commission, the 1901 national census identified Eli Roy as a Roman Catholic "French Breed" whose mother tongue was Cree but who had three years of schooling and could write English and French.[52] Given that individuals of that era did not have Social Insurance Numbers or driver's licences with picture identification, signatures are of interest because they were often the only identity markers available. Roy's signature on the application (Figure 4) seems consistent with an individual possessing some education, as the application signature is likely in his own hand. In subsequent documents, Roy's signature does not reappear; instead, the mark of an X appears with his name. Individual scrip grantees are identified in the various records that make up the paper trail. On his "Half-breed" certificate Roy was identified as "Eli Roy son of Francis Roy" (Figure 6), and on the coupon issue order and both coupons he was identified with the same wording (Figures 7, 1, and 2). Subsequently, the expression "Eli Roy son of Francis Roy" appeared on the conveyance instruments (Figures 9 and 10) and on the applications for Homestead Lands.[53] Clearly, all the available information required to present another individual as a grantee was already on the face of the coupon, which was in possession of those involved in the conversion of the coupon into title.

Nevertheless, a certain Alex L'Esperance stepped forward to identify Eli Roy at both the Humboldt and Moose Jaw Dominion Land Offices.[54] So far, our database information indicates that Alex L'Esperance's signature appeared as a witness on fifty conveyance instruments, and on the reverse sides of forty-eight land scrip coupons.[55] Between 15 March 1906 and 18 July 1911, L'Esperance identified coupon-holders at the Battleford, Saskatoon, Humboldt, Regina, Estevan, Moose Jaw, Medicine Hat, and Calgary Dominion Land Offices. Unless he was inclined to hang out at various Dominion Land Offices, it would appear that the identification of Métis grantees at Dominion Land Offices was an organized operation. Nevertheless, possible discrepancies in signatures and marks highlight problems with the conveyance of scrip interests.

At this point we have some nagging doubts about the compliance with the Rule of Location. For one, it would have taken a Métis person from the Claim Region several days, in the most ideal conditions, to travel from Northwest Saskatchewan to a Dominion Land Office in order to locate and register his scrip and then assign his interests to lands he would never see.[56] Given that the conversion of scrip into land largely involved land speculators, the Métis grantee had no practical role to play. Significantly, the grantee was not operating as land speculator with the profit motive to flip parcels of scrip/homestead lands; the grantee is therefore not needed to select the land and, at any rate, held little knowledge of local land markets with which to select the most desirable lands. Apart from the need to comply with the Rule of Location, the Métis grantee had no necessary role to play in the conversion of paper to land.

It was also potentially somewhat costly to transport grantees to Dominion Land Offices. Alluding to the cost of travel in a different situation, N.O. Cote wrote to Deputy Minister A.M. Burgess that a grantee lived "seventy-five miles west of Edmonton, and to bring her to Calgary and take her back would cost as much as the scrip is worth."[57] The difficulty with complying with the Rule of Location was also revealed by the experiences of a young Winnipeg law student, William Parker Fillmore, who had participated in scrip buying during the Treaty Ten Commission in 1906. Much later he recorded his memories of this process:

> I have always wondered how the buyer, or purchaser, of scrip from him, got title...which the person named in the scrip was entitled to get, by attending at a Dominion Land Office, and locating the scrip.... It would have been a matter of considerable difficulty to go north and find the person named in the scrip and bring him out to the Land Office. I have a hazy memory that the buyers, when purchasing the scrip, would have the vendor sign a form of Quit Claim Deed. He would sign by making his mark, and this would be witnessed by two persons, presumably other dealers (Fillmore 128).[58]

Here Fillmore identifies the purchaser of the scrip as responsible for making the arrangements to comply with the Rule of the Location. Further, Fillmore explains how the difficulties of arranging the participation of northern grantees were overcome:

> After my return to Winnipeg I made some inquiries, and I was told that the practice was for the holder of a scrip to pick out some local Indian or half-breed and take him to the Dominion Land Office and present him as the person named in the scrip. The holder of the scrip, pretending to be the agent of the half-breed, would designate the land. The patent to this land would then be issued, and the scrip holder would then have to get title. Presumably, this was done by completing and registering the Quit Claim Deed. (Fillmore 128)

Given the logistical difficulties outlined above, and the fact that grantees were not holding their coupons, motives and opportunities not to comply with the Rule of Location clearly existed.

Signature discrepancies, costly travel barriers, and third-party possession of scrip coupons support Fillmore's statement that Métis grantees were impersonated in order to circumvent the Rule of Location. If impersonation was widespread, then the establishment of "good title" was uncertain in this era. Knowledge of such impersonation generates a "cloud on title."[59] And if many of the lands obtained with land scrip were problematic, a very large cloud would have been cast over the prairie landscape.

In fact, the impersonation of a grantee for the purpose of obtaining a patent, as reported by Fillmore, was not a minor transgression in the early twentieth century. Several sections of the *Criminal Code* (1910) dealt with property frauds. For example, section 408 "Personation with intent to obtain property" states that "Every one is guilty of an indictable offence and liable to fourteen years' imprisonment, who, with intent fraudulently to obtain any property, personates any person, living or dead...."[60] In section 468 "Punishment for forgery," the scope of forgery in relationship to property is established. Several examples of forged documents would seem to have been relevant to the Rule of Location and the assignment or conveyance of land scrip interests, including "(c) any document containing evidence of, or forming the title or any part of the title...; (d) any entry in any register or book; (e) any document required for the purpose of procuring the registering of any such title;...(o) any power of attorney or other authority to transfer any interest;...(s) *any scrip* in lieu of land...is guilty of an indictable offence and liable to IMPRISONMENT FOR LIFE if the document forged purports to be, or was intended by the offender to be understood to be or to be used as genuine."[61] The inclusion of "any scrip in lieu of land" suggests that Métis scrip coupons were something more than a mere piece of chattel. Clearly, with sentences ranging from fourteen years to life imprisonment, violation of the individual interest in property was punishable.

Despite severe punishment for such offenses, Métis scrip grantees do not appear to have been protected against impersonation and forgery.[62] On 1 June 1921, Bill 138, a bill to amend the Criminal Code was itself abruptly amended in the Senate. Section 1140 of the Criminal Code imposed time limitations for the prosecution of several offences, and it was amended so that "Any offence relating to or arising out of the location of land which was paid for in whole or in part by scrip or was granted upon certificates issued to half-breeds in connection with extinguishment of Indian title" could not be prosecuted after three years from the occurrence of the offense.[63] Prior to this amendment, section 1140 was largely aimed at treason and moral crimes. On 21 June 1922, Senator Sir James Lougheed read aloud in the Senate Chamber a letter from the Parliamentary Counsel Francis R. Gisborne justifying the amendment: "It is urged that there were a good many irregularities amounting to fraud and perjury in connection with the location of these lands, and parties are raking up these frauds for the purpose of blackmail."[64] If the Parliamentary Counsel is a reliable authority, then Fillmore's report on impersonation of scrip grantees and the lack of support for compliance with the Rule of Location gains additional and official support. Moreover, the justification advanced by Gisborne and Lougheed indicates a greater concern about the blackmailing of scrip buyers than the property frauds ("irregularities") associated with the interests of Métis grantees.

As of yet, we have not found an instance in which the Parliament of Canada placed similar time limits on prosecutions with respect to frauds or forgeries for any other category of the many land tenures arising out of the Dominion Lands Act. The concern of Parliament would seem to have been somewhat selective. The effect of this amendment was to decriminalize scrip frauds arising out of the relationship between the Crown and the Métis in respect to Aboriginal title.

Parting Considerations

Without the specific research needs generated by the Métis claim to Northwest Saskatchewan, the history of scrip would have pretty much remained as it was. While it is understandable that the academy would be reluctant to accord any credibility to "adversarial" claims research, this activity does affect the Ivory Tower.[65] Clearly, the position taken today by government officials and advocates claiming that the scrip system successfully ended Métis interests in Aboriginal title is an invitation to inquire into some rather obscure corners of Canadian history. Our investigation into the scrip system suggests that many historical complications potentially confound the broad legal assertions about the effect of scrip on Aboriginal title.

The reasons why scrip became integral to the settlement frontier and yet at odds with intrinsic principles (good title, lawful assignments, orderly conveyances, reliable registration of interests) of the very property foundation that colonialism was seeking to establish requires an analysis informed by the precepts of political economy and historical geography that is beyond the scope of this paper. Once the individual cases of Métis grantees "selling" scrip certificates to buyers who in turn converted paper into land are identified and compiled, the general discharge of property will be understood. For now, the capacity of the scrip system to promote the commercialization of public homestead lands is clear: under the scrip system, public lands regulated by the Dominion Lands Act were privatized and entered the sphere of the market, meeting a demand for land by farmers, ranchers, agents, and developers. Under the guise of an acknowledgment of Métis entitlement to lands, the government implemented a system that facilitated western settlement and, in a few cases, the accumulation of wealth.

Although it is somewhat provisional, our counter-story of Métis scrip was arrived at through tedious examination of archival documents and emerges as a series of connected stories, or as pieces of a larger, still unfolding account. Each document, usually generated in response to a previous document, involves its own cast of individuals. Linking documents, made feasible by database technology, allows us to connect the individuals, resulting in a rather eclectic group of investments and motives working within the larger colonial scheme and, more particularly, the National Policy of the Canadian government. In a certain sense, Eli Roy has been rescued from the obscurity of official history; because this research relates to a present-day land claim and also to contentious and polarized views about the past treatment of Aboriginal peoples, Roy and many more Métis will be re-instated as representatives of a historically significant people.

Following the treaties between the Crown and First Nations, a system of property with an efficient surveying system and a host of tenures and grants to register these private grants transformed the organization of geographical space. Indeed, for the Métis, the rights to the land appear to have been transferred. In a certain sense, the scrip system was a collision of two property systems. Aboriginal systems of tenure, as described by Peter Usher, are characterized as communal, a form of social property in which resource harvesting and management create a unified system that promotes conservation (Usher 38–44). To a large extent, the failure of both the scrip system and treaties to accommodate this system of tenure as settlement and development encroached is fundamental to the current land and resource conflicts. Recently, in *R. v. Blais*, the Supreme Court of Canada provided this comment on the scrip system:

> The perceived differences between the Crown's obligations
> to Indians and its relationship with the Métis was reflected in
> separate arrangements for the distribution of land. Different legal
> and political regimes governed the conclusion of Indian treaties
> and the allocation of Métis scrip. Indian treaties were concluded
> on a collective basis and entailed collective rights, whereas
> scrip entitled recipients to individual grants of land. While the
> history of *scrip speculation and devaluation is a sorry chapter in our
> nation's history*, this does not change the fact that scrip was based
> on fundamentally different assumptions about the nature and
> origins of the government's relationship with scrip recipients
> than the assumptions underlying treaties with Indians.[66]

Such a fundamental assumption about the government's historical relationship with the Métis might prove to be constrained by the realization that the scrip system could be justified not as a loss of lands available for settlement, but as a gain. Once comprehensively researched, this chapter in Canada's history may end up being sorrier than the Supreme Court could ever have imagined. As this article suggests, the problem is not simply a serious difference (devaluation) between the price paid for scrip and the value of land that could be obtained with a coupon or even that such prospects attracted "speculators"; rather, claims to equity, fairness, and impartiality of the scrip system may be challenged. Widespread impersonation of land scrip grantees cannot be justified by the assertion that the government did not want to deal with the Métis as it had done with the Indians. Ultimately, it might turn out to be an even worse breach of justice if the courts determine that the Métis, with respect to their land interests, were entitled neither to the Crown's protection enjoyed by Indians nor to the property rights that the Anglo legal system provided to "Europeans."

Our initial reconstruction of a trail of documents reveals that the scrip system was, at best, a curious attempt to mesh two notions about property—an Indian title that had to be extinguished and a European system of varied tenures and specific rights—but which promoted fee simple title in a frontier prairie region where a system of land registry had just been laid down. Of course, it is hard to imagine how all this might really have succeeded for the Métis and, in the long run, it may have, apart from a small group of scrip buyers, failed for all concerned.

Acknowledgements

We would like to acknowledge the many individuals who have worked on the matriX project since 1999, most of whom were students at the time of their involvement. The collective endeavours of these individuals have led us to a better understanding and appreciation of the Halfbreed Scrip process. Converting archival documents into database records is tedious and often mind-numbing work. During the early years of the project, Anna Ryding, Kevin MacLennan, Clayton "Buster" Leonard, Nonnie Jackson, Sara Cardinal, and Katie Morrison, in particular, provided dedicated contributions to the project. More recently, Katherin McArdle also provided valuable assistance. We also benefited from the interest shown by Clem Chartier, Jean Tiellet, Jason Madden and Douglas Kovatch, all lawyers. The support of the Métis Nation–Saskatchewan, Métis National Council, and the University of Alberta has made this work possible. The interpretations, along with the errors and mistakes, are our own and do not represent the views of the University of Alberta, Métis National Council, the Northwest Saskatchewan Métis Council Land Claim Committee, or the Métis—Nation Saskatchewan.

NOTES

1 Gerald Morin et al., Métis Nation of Saskatchewan, "Statement of Claim" Queen's Bench No. 619, Judicial Centre of Saskatoon, SK (1994). The Claim Region includes lands north of Meadow Lake, south of Lake Athabasca, west of the Alberta/Saskatchewan border and east towards approximately 105°w longitude.
2 The Supreme Court of Canada in the recent Powley decision recognized the Métis as Aboriginal people with Aboriginal rights. See R. v. Powley 2003 Supreme Court of Canada 43, File No. 28533.
3 Aboriginal title is regarded as unique or special. The Supreme Court of Canada has defined Aboriginal title as "sui generis, and so distinguished from other proprietary interests, and characterized by several dimensions. It is inalienable and cannot be transferred, sold or surrendered to anyone other than the Crown. Another dimension of aboriginal title is its sources: its recognition by the Royal Proclamation, 1763 and the relationship between the common law which recognizes occupation as proof of possession and systems of aboriginal law pre-existing assertion of British sovereignty. Finally, aboriginal title is held communally." Delgamuukw v. British Columbia [1997] 3 S.C.R. 1010, [1997] S.C.J. No. 108 (preamble). An accessible source for this judgment is The Supreme Court of Canada Decision on Aboriginal Title: Delgamuukw.
4 For an informative summary of Métis rights, see Canada, Report of the Royal Commission on Aboriginal Peoples: Perspectives and Realities, 4:199–386.
5 For the details on the significance of the events of 1870, see Frank Tough, "Aboriginal Rights Versus the Deed of Surrender: The Legal Rights of Native Peoples and Canada's Acquisition of the Hudson's Bay Company Territory."
6 For a history of this region based on genealogical archival sources, see Brenda MacDougall, "Socio-Cultural Development and Identity Formation of Métis Communities in Northwestern Saskatchewan, 1776–1907."
7 In the 1901 national census, the Native population of this region was almost entirely identified as "Breeds," National Archives of Canada, Record Group 31, Census of 1901, Microfilm Reel T6555 (hereafter NAC, RG 31). In 1906, a total of 394 Indians were paid by Commissioner J.A.J. McKenna, compared to the 546 individual claims for scrip in the same year. See Canada, Treaty No. 10 and Reports of Commissioners, 9; and NAC, RG 15, vol. 1515, Claims Register.
8 On the migration from Red River, see Gerhard J. Ens, Homeland to Hinterland: The Changing World of the Red River Metis in the Nineteenth Century; Gerhard J. Ens, "Dispossession or Adaptation? Migration and Persistence of the Red River Metis, 1835–1890"; and P.R. Mailhot and D.N. Sprague, "Persistent Settlers: The Dispersal and Resettlement of the Red River Metis, 1870–1885."

9 A.A. Seaborne, "A Population Geography of North Saskatchewan."

10 On the question of the significance of the fur trade to the development of Canada, see Harold A. Innis, *The Fur Trade In Canada: An Introduction to Canadian Economic History* and its introductory essay by Arthur J. Ray.

11 Northern Saskatchewan Métis communities, under the auspices of the Northwest Saskatchewan Métis Council, have been conducting training and research in the area of traditional land-use studies.

12 Kevin MacLennan suggested the name "matriX." For an introduction to the matriX Project, see Linda Goyette, "Land Grab: The X files."

13 For an overview, see Peter J. Usher, Frank Tough and Robert M. Galois, "Reclaiming the Land: Aboriginal Title, Treaty Rights and Land Claims in Canada."

14 The Dominion government issued scrip and warrants redeemable in western Canadian lands to particular groups, including the original white settlers, those who served with the militia under Colonel Wolseley, the North-West Mounted Police, the militia forces in North-West in 1885, and the South African Volunteers. These western grants had been preceded in the pre-confederation era for Upper Canada by scrip issued to members of the militia and United Empire Loyalists. Money scrip could also be used as payment to secure other types of Dominion land tenures and titles.

15 On homestead policies, see James M. Richtik, "Competition for Settlers, The Canadian Viewpoint"; James M. Richtik, "The Policy Framework for Settling the Canadian West, 1870–1880"; and Kirk N. Lambrecht, *The Administration of Dominion Lands, 1870–1930*.

16 In the Claim Region, successful claimants were granted 240 acres of land scrip or 240 dollars of money scrip. Since the Dominion Lands survey system allotted lands in 160-acre quarter sections and 80 acres or halves of a quarter sections, the grant of two coupons of 160 and 80 acres each would conform to the geometry of the survey system. Coupons of less than the normal value were issued to heirs who shared in the award to a deceased claimant.

17 The Department of the Interior sold lands closer to railways at a higher price than the average price of homestead lands.

18 Scrip coupons were purchased by private interests, not the government, but the Interior Department redeemed both land and money scrip from interested parties as a means of paying for land and other tenures. If the cash received by the Métis grantee is regarded as compensation for Indian title, then it is important to note that compensation was paid out by private interests and not the Crown.

19 One estimate indicates that Northwest Halfbreed grants of money scrip amounted to $2,095,817, compared to a land scrip total of 1,161,612 acres. Thus 35.6 percent of the total was land scrip. The amount of Métis scrip lands was much less than the Dominion Lands allocated to railway interests or the Hudson's Bay Company; however, this form of grant was not irrelevant to prairie settlement history. This figure does not include the grants of land and scrip for the Red River Settlement in Manitoba, ca. 1870. See N.O. Cote, "Administration and Sale of Dominion Lands, Claims Under the Manitoba Act, Half-Breed Claims and Letters Patent for Dominion Lands, 1871–1930," copy found in NAC, RG 15, vol. 38, file 2. See also Frank Tough, "Activities of Metis Scrip Commissions," 61–62.

20 Chain of title is defined as "Successive conveyances, or other forms of alienation, affecting a particular parcel of land, arranged consecutively, from the government or original source down to the present holder" (Black 290).

21 Beginning in 1907, scrip commissioners no longer approved claims "in country" by issuing certificates. Also around this time, coupons were delivered personally to the grantee after the validity of the claim had been determined in Ottawa.

22 The scrip issued under the *Manitoba Act* and in the scrip commissions in the late 1880s would only approximate this particular representation. Money scrip was a simpler process.

23 Under the authority of a statute, Orders-in-Council carry the force of law and are a mechanism for implementing the more general provisions of a statute. Beginning with the 1889 territorial adhesion to Treaty Six, treating with the Indians and taking scrip claims were simultaneous. The scrip commission of 1885, 1886, and 1887 covered lands "ceded" in the treaties of the 1870s. With Treaty Ten and the Adhesion to Treaty Five, a single commissioner served to treat with the Indians and to approve scrip claims.

24 Where and when claimants were born were important factors. Also, commissioners would reject claims if a claimant had already received scrip from an earlier commission. Claims with some merit, but which had not been anticipated by the exact criteria established by the Order-in-Council, would be considered by the Ottawa staff of the Department of the Interior.

25 An appreciation for the difference between certificates and scrip coupons or notes is essential, but often this distinction is not obvious in the correspondence records of the Department of the Interior.

26 Neither coupon had to be converted at the same time or in the same land office. "Open" homestead lands were surveyed, unoccupied, and set aside for homesteading. Land lying outside of the belt of land surveyed by Dominion land surveyors or lands set aside for railroad companies or other interests within the surveyed townships were not available. Scrip coupons could not be applied to unsurveyed lands because the township/range survey system was the basis for allocating homestead lands. The process was similar to a prospective settler selecting a parcel of open homestead lands. For a comparison of scrip and homestead procedures, see Kevin MacLennan, "For the 'Purposes of the Dominion': Métis Entitlement and the Regulatory Regime of 'Halfbreed' Scrip."

27 Typescript copy of a section of Bulletin No. 21 (2 January 1930) Department of the Interior, copy found in Archives of Manitoba, Record Group 17, Box 89, B1, File 17.2.1, 19 November 1931. However, a process known as "Redbacking" permitted the locating of the coupon without the presence of the grantee. See Frank Tough and Leah Dorion, "'The Claims of the Halfbreeds...Have Been Finally Closed'": A Study of Treaty Ten and Treaty Five Adhesion Scrip."

28 According to Black's Law Dictionary, good title is "free from all encumbrances. A title which on the record itself can be again sold as free from obvious defects and substantial doubts...." Good title "differs from 'good marketable title,' which is an actual title, but which may be established by evidence independent of the record"(Black 353).

29 For an analysis of the advantages of orderly title registration over costs and defects of private conveyances, see S. Rowton Simpson, Land Law and Registration.

30 For example, NAC, RG 15, liber 329, folio 158, fiat number 167580 granting lands to C.C. Hague on 4 January 1909. Also on the Letter Patent is the notation that N.O. Cote had recorded the grant on 5 January 1909.

31 This literature tends to privilege the official narrative of the way the process was supposed to work, often overlooking the discrepancies revealed through detailed archival research. See, for instance, D.J. Hall, "The Half-Breed Claims Commission"; D.N. Sprague, "The Manitoba Land Question, 1870–1882"; D.N. Sprague, "Government Lawlessness in the Administration of Manitoba Land Claims, 1870–1887"; Joe Sawchuk, Patricia Sawchuk, and Theresa Ferguson, Metis Land Rights in Alberta: A Political History, 87–158; Ken Hatt, "The Northwest Scrip Commissions as Federal Policy: Some Initial Findings"; Ken Hatt, "North-West Rebellion Scrip Commissions, 1885–1889"; Thomas Flanagan, "Comment on Ken Hatt, 'The North-West Rebellion Scrip Commissions, 1885–1889'"; Thomas Flanagan, "The Market for Métis Lands in Manitoba: An Exploratory Study"; and Thomas Flanagan and Gerhard Ens, "Metis Land Grants in Manitoba: A Statistical Summary."

32 This became known as Treaty Ten. See PC 1459 (20 July 1906) copy found in NAC, RG 15, vol. 227, part 5.

33 We can only wonder how the Métis of this era reacted to this unprecedented, intrusive data collection by a group of official-looking strangers. Today, however, these records, which are more detailed than the band annuity pay-lists for Treaty Indians kept by the Department of Indian Affairs, provide much demographic information about Métis individuals and communities. Since many applications record personal information on three generations of Métis, and since married women were required to provide information on separate declarations, these details help researchers reconstruct some of the social history of the Métis and the historical Métis Nation. Today such data can assist with the individual need to meet verifiable and objective criteria concerning connections to Métis ancestry and Métis communities.

34 The duplicate copy of his certificate retained by the Department of the Interior is found in NAC, RG 15, vol. 1384, Scrip Certificates, H No. 137.

35 Note that the certificate indicates that the grantee is the individual who redeems the coupon. Roy's certificates are found in NAC, RG 15, vol. 1008, file 1463735; and NAC, RG 15, vol. 1384.

36 NAC, RG 15, vol. 1008, file 1463775, Boulton to Keyes (27 September 1907).

37 NAC, RG 15, vol. 1008, file 1463775, Keyes to Boulton (3 October 1907); and NAC, RG 15, vol. 1520, Delivery Register.

38 NAC, RG 15, vol. 1008, file 1463775, Boulton to Keyes (15 October 1907).

39 See NAC, RG 15, vols. 1518, 1519 and 1520, Delivery Registers.

40 Saskatchewan Archives Board, Homestead File 1908546, Application to purchase SE 1/4 of section 13, township 32, range 26 west of the second meridian (25 November 1919) (hereafter SAB).

41 NAC, RG 15, vol., 1548, Location Register; and SAB, Homestead File 1698842, Application to purchase N 1/2 of SE 1/4 of section 1, township 11, range 5 west of the third meridian (13 January 1910).

42 SAB, Homestead File 1908546, Walch to Department of the Interior (25 February 1910). The letterhead on the correspondence accompanying the Quit Claim Deed depicted "The Walch Land Co. Lands-Mortgages-Investments."

43 See NAC, RG 15, vol. 1547, Location Register; NAC, RG 15, Land Patent, liber 406, folio 117, patent fiat 198901; and on 5 April 1910 Walch was advised by Perley G. Keyes, Secretary, Department of the Interior, that his patent had been issued on 22 March 1910 and that it had been forwarded to the Registrar of Land Registration District of Saskatoon, SAB, Homestead File 1908546.

44 SAB, Homestead File 1698842, Application 13 January 1910.

45 See NAC, RG 15, vol. 1548 location register; and NAC, RG 15, Land Patent, liber 398, folio 89, patent fiat 195303.

46 As of 1933, 10 coupons were unredeemed and 4 coupons had missing information. Based on an analysis of data in NAC, RG 15, vols. 1539–1550, Location Registers.

47 How officials responded to allegations of non-compliance with the Rule of Location and/ or questionable conveyances of the grantee's interests is another important feature of the implementation of the scrip system, but space does not permit consideration here.

48 Two fundamental references on the question of Aboriginal land interests surviving the advent of European systems of property are the Royal Proclamation of 7 October 1763 and an Imperial Order-in-Council of Her Majesty in Council admitting Rupert's Land and the North-Western Territory into the Union (23 June 1870).

49 Based on an analysis of NAC, RG 15, vols. 1518–1520, Delivery Registers.

50 Fourteen coupons were delivered to the Claim Region and the Adjacent Treaty Territory. Based on an analysis of NAC, RG 15, vols. 1518–1520, Delivery Registers.

51 In instances when two groups of scrip buyers claimed ownership of the same coupon, problems ensued when the coupon was delivered to one of the competing parties. The

Department of the Interior abandoned this delivery procedure in 1907 and had the coupons delivered to the grantees.

52 NAC, RG 31, Census of Canada, 1901, Reel T 6555. Three years of schooling would not equip anyone to read and understand the conveyance instruments; however, this would seem to be more education than many Aboriginal people received in that day and region.

53 "Eli Roy, son of Francis" appears in the records generated for the locating of scrip; see SAB, Homestead File 1908546, Application 25 November 1909; and SAB, Homestead File 1698842, Application 13 January 1910.

54 Alex L'Esperance (also Alexis and Alexander) identified Roy on the backs of Land Scrip Coupons A8770 and A9809.

55 Based on 1727 records of land scrip coupons, NAC, RG 15, vols. 1406 to 1410, Land Scrip; and records for 5477 transfer documents (assignments) from NAC, RG 15 vols. 1430–1474, Land Assignments.

56 Scrip coupons could only be used to purchase land in surveyed territory. The Claim Region had not been surveyed into townships at the time scrip was in circulation. Location for their own use would have meant the Métis grantee would have had to relocate from a region in which their community had been well established for many years. Further, the Northwest Saskatchewan economy was based largely on fishing and hunting, so relocating to the southern surveyed lands would have necessitated an economic shift and risk.

57 NAC, RG 15, vol. 708, file 360372, N.O. Cote to A.M. Burgess (15 July 1894).

58 W.P. Fillmore, QC, practised law following his call to the Bar in 1907 until his retirement in 1972; he practised with Bradshaw, Richardson, and Affleck, later with Richards, Affleck, Kemp, and Fillmore, and still later with Fillmore, Riley. He served on the executive of the Canadian Bar Association (1943–1944), as a Bencher of the Law Society of Manitoba (1946–1948) and as President of the Manitoba Bar Association (1946–1948). See obituary of William Parker Fillmore Q.C., *Manitoba Tribune*, 7 May 1978.

59 An important concept in the context of scrip assignments, "cloud on title" is defined as "[a]n outstanding claim or incumbrance which, if valid, would affect or impair the title of the owner of a particular estate, and on its face has that effect, but can be shown by extrinsic proof to be invalid or inapplicable to the estate in question. A conveyance, mortgage, judgment, tax-levy, etc., may all, in proper cases, constitute a cloud on title" (Black 322). A cloud on title indicates uncertainty about the legitimacy of ownership of a piece of property or parcel of land (estate). If a grantee's scrip interest had been improperly conveyed to another party, then the validity of title is in question.

60 *Criminal Code*, 1910, Revised Statutes of Canada, 1906, c.146, s.408.

61 *Criminal Code*, 1910, R.S.C., 1906, c.146, s.469 [upper case in original, emphasis added].

62 In 1916, the Exchequer Court of Canada held that land scrip was chattel. See L'Hirondelle (Antoine) v. *The King*, [1916] 16 Exchequer Court of Canada Reports, pp. 193–195 and L'Hirondelle (Joseph) v. *The King*, [1916] EX.C.R. at p. 196–198. These decisions are published in Brian Slattery and Linda Charlton, eds., *Canadian Native Law Cases: 1911–1930* vol. 4:258–265; they are also available online: http://library.usask.ca/native/cnlc/volo4/258.html and http://library.usask.ca/native/cnlc/volo4/258.html.

63 The amendment occurred during Committee of the Whole Government of Canada, *Debates of the Senate of the Dominion of Canada*: 1921, 720–721). On this issue, see also Sawchuk, Sawchuk, and Ferguson 148–151.

64 Government of Canada, *Debates of the Senate*: 1922, 500, indicating correspondence from Francis H. Gisborne to Sir James Lougheed (31 May 1920).

65 For further discussion, see Arthur J. Ray, "Aboriginal Title and Treaty Rights Research: A Comparative Look at Australia, Canada, New Zealand and the United States"; and Arthur J. Ray, "Native History on Trial: Confessions of an Expert Witness."

66 R. v. *Blais*, *Supreme Court Reporter*, 2003, paragraph 34 (neutral citation 2003 S.C.C. 44. File
    28645) [emphasis added]. This comment does not provide any additional context, and it
    is important to realize that there are differences between the scrip issued in relation to the
    Manitoba Act and the scrip provided by the *Dominion Lands Act*.

FOUR

NATION-BUILDING AS PROCESS

Reflections of a Nihiyow [Cree]

Harold Cardinal

AFTER LISTENING to the presentations all day long, I feel almost as if I were at one of those really fine, classy restaurants facing a large and diverse buffet, and not quite knowing what to pick from. Rather than deciding what topic from these presentations to comment on, I'll comment instead on matters that weren't discussed at length. First, I wanted to express my appreciation for the invitation to participate. I particularly enjoyed our American guest's [Patricia Seed's] presentation because I think there are a number of areas where that presentation, as well as the others, are relevant to what is happening in Indian country today.[1]

I have, for the last twenty years or so, been engaged as a full-time student, studying, on the one hand, under the direction and guidance of traditional teachers from Cree and other First Nations and, on the other, more recently, at various universities. My studies have focussed in part on trying to discover the points at which there might be convergences between the knowledge systems of the Cree people and other First Nations and the knowledge systems found in Western educational institutions.

We need to recognize that the colonizing experience has been pervasive and extensive throughout both the Aboriginal community and the white community.[2] One of the things I found informative in Patricia Seed's talk is that, from an intellectual point of view, perhaps some of us in the First Nations communities make the conceptual mistake, when we use the term "white man," of assuming that we are dealing with a uniform whiteness or sameness when discussing the "white community." As is sometimes the case when First Nation communities are described, there is the tendency to ascribe a uniform sameness to them without acknowledgement of their diverse linguistic, cultural, or traditional differences.

The consequence is often that not enough attention is given to the differences existing in the intellectual or traditional histories of both white peoples and First Nations.

I was also interested in the distinction our American guest made between the conception of human rights as an individual rights paradigm contrasted to the other more collective formulations of the human rights paradigm. I say this, making more of a mental note to myself in terms of where we have to go in forging a different direction for the future of First Nations peoples. First Nations peoples today are being required to step back and assess what has been happening across the country and within our communities. In our assessment process, some of us are beginning to realize how much we have internalized or adopted, as First Nations or Aboriginal peoples, the colonial mindset of government bureaucrats, policy makers, and law makers. This statement is not intended to be value-laden or a diatribe against Euro-colonialism. Rather, my statement is made in an effort to recognize the scope and complexity of the task our peoples are facing in their nation-building undertakings today. This task requires that we look at ourselves not only as individuals but as members of the communities from which we originate, and that we understand clearly, honestly, and accurately what is happening in and to our communities.

One of the initial challenges in the nation-building exercise is the need for a careful analysis of the many issues underlying the question of identity. I only have time here to outline some matters that need urgent attention and resolution, though we need to return at another time to review the issues in more detail. In dealing with the question of identity, Cree Elders pose the following question to their young people: *"Awina maga kee anow."* In translation this says, "Who is it that we really are?" The Elders pose this question in their own language and context in a way that resonates in a broader environment.

Colonization is not an experience unique to the Cree or other First Nations. It is an experience we share with other Canadians and with other peoples throughout the world. In this context, the term "colonization" is intended to be descriptive rather than definitive. It is descriptive in the sense that it describes a historical reality in Canada and other parts of the world. That reality is simply this: European nations sent their peoples to different parts of the world where they established colonies. Through these colonies, European nations occupied and assumed control over territories and peoples of those lands. In 1867, Great Britain reorganized its European colonies located in Canada under one government. That reorganization was effected in 1867 with the passage of the British North

America Act in the British Parliament. Though it gave some governance rights to its colonies, Britain retained continuing control of its British colony. Canada did not receive its full and complete independence as a nation-state until the patriation of the British North America Act in 1982. Hence, for Aboriginal and non-Aboriginal peoples, the process of decolonization and nation-building is a continuing one in Canada.

Other nations throughout the world are still in the process of nation-building. We see this in a contemporary context in countries like post-apartheid South Africa or the new nations that emerged after the break-up of the Soviet Union or in the struggle of Palestinians to create their own state. Even in nations, like Israel, that achieved independence in the mid-1950s, we see a continuing process of giving secular states a meaning related to identity. There, the Israeli Supreme Court had to consider the question of "Who is a Jew?" Here in Canada, I would dare say that Canadians, in different regions of the country, are still trying to formulate an answer or answers to the question of "what is a Canadian?" or "who is it that 'Canadians' really are?" In that sense, the questions other peoples ask themselves are not that different from that posed by Cree Elders to their young people. For Aboriginal persons, the question of identity is made more complicated and difficult by the particular historical treatment to which First Nations peoples were subjected in Canada. Today, these questions signal a particular phase of decolonization. As such, it is becoming clear to more and more Aboriginal persons that the answers must be found within and among the people who constitute the particular nation. Legitimate answers can no longer be provided by some omnipotent power located in foreign jurisdictions outside the context of the particular peoples concerned.

In Canada, Europeans arrogated unto themselves the power and authority to determine and define who was and was not a Cree person or who was or was not a member of a First Nation.[3] The identities of Cree and other First Nations peoples were to be determined by a legal construct. That legal construct began with a legal presumption that Crees and other First Nations peoples were primitive, savage, and heathen, and hence not possessing the capacity to be recognized as persons under the laws of the country. Public policy was predicated on the assumption that public good would best be advanced by removing Crees and other First Nations peoples from their "wilderness habitations" and relocating them to places where they could be "isolated from their past" and protected from "contamination," from the influence of premature contact with "civilization." They were to be "civilized and Christianized" in a carefully controlled and legally secured environment. These places were conceived as "half-way house" laboratories in which Crees and other First Nations peoples were to be sanitized, civilized, and Christianized. The goal of Canadian public policy and law was that once the Crees and other First Nations peoples completed the transformative process, they were to emerge into Canadian society, free from their wild and primitive past, inculcated with a sense of self-shame so strongly embedded that they would never again yearn for or seek to be associated with their former "savage" identities.

This legal construct became entrenched in Canadian law and public policy in determining who an "Indian" was and who had a legal right to be a member of the group known as "Indians." By arrogating these powers unto themselves, Europeans sought to possess the exclusive power to determine who was and was not an Indian; who was entitled to inhabit Indian communities; and who could or could not be entitled to receive state services and recognition. The labels that Europeans adopted for the Cree and other First Nations, such as "heathens," "savages," or "rude and primitive men," reflected a particular time and era of European history when the world and its inhabitants were divided into those who were "civilized" and those who were not, those who were Christian and those who were not. There is no clearer description of the European mandate to civilize, Christianize, and dominate others than that expressed by Judge Boyd in the St. Catherine's Milling and Lumber Case of 1885. In that case, Boyd described the Indians of Ontario and Western Canada as "rude and primitive men" who needed to be civilized and through civilization transformed into "productive members of civilized societies."[4]

Though decolonization requires the deconstruction of these racist colonial paradigms, we are confronted with the effects and consequence of a centuries-old, carefully constructed, state-sponsored system designed to transform the minds and souls of all First Nations persons in Canada. For decades upon decades it was the only system imposed and enforced upon the First Nations peoples. This became for many the only reality known by successive generations, and it was this reality that pervasively informed all thoughts respecting the question of collective identity and individual self-identity. Those who sought to maintain their tribal languages, customs, cultures, or connections became the objects of state-inspired and -encouraged ostracism. Those who sought to maintain and strengthen their original identity became, over time, the minority who were characterized as the small, backward remnants of a radical minority, yearning to return to a distant past to which they could never return.

Canadian laws were enacted to enforce this paradigm. Successive generations of First Nations children were removed from their families and communities and taken to places where they could be isolated from the world so that those who sought to re-frame and transform their minds and souls could do so in complete and unabridged freedom. Laws mandated the separation of families from one another and authorized the forced removal of whole families from their communities. These same laws made it illegal for those removed to return to live in their communities of origin. These laws became the only basis for determining who could be considered an Indian and who had or did not have the right to live with and among the Indians.

This history of state labelling has had a pervasive effect on First Nations people collectively and individually. They were forced by the laws of Canada, decade after decade, to accept the removal of their brothers, sisters, sons, and daughters from their communities without any recourse. Over a long period of time, for an increasing number of First Nations people, this removal was the norm and the law to be followed. Such assimilationist strategies, encouraged under the Indian Act, shaped the legal standards that determined Indian identity and membership in Canada. Even after the 1985 amendments to the Indian Act, this Act still controls and limits the persons who can be recognized under its laws. We are confronted with a situation rooted in a long colonial history and legal practice where a state government possesses not only the sole right and power to label First Nations peoples with a particular identity, but also the authority to keep redefining that label to the extent that the issue of identity keeps going around in an endless circle, causing havoc, pain, and suffering in our communities. I look, for example, at the state power exercised through the Indian Act in defining who is an Indian, the number of times that definition has changed, the consequence in terms of the hundreds, thousands of people who were one day considered Indian under the laws of the country and then, the next day, considered non-Indian by those same laws without anything having changed except a legal definition. And then I see the internal division and strife that results from those changes. It is a strife that rips apart families in Indian country.

The most recent manifestation is found in the Bill C-31 debate across the country. One finds thousands of individuals who have gained or regained state recognition of their status through the provisions of the Indian Act. Yet many of these individuals continue to find themselves at the outskirts of their communities of origin. Persons in their communities are saying, "We don't want you back." An increasing number of these excluded individuals are finding themselves in a legal twilight zone; while they have achieved legal recognition, they are discovering that it remains, in substance, a fraudulent mirage. They have succeeded in acquiring a legal label, but it is one to which few if any rights or benefits flow. It is one that does not allow them to become members of a community nor entitle them to the benefits that flow to those members of the community. This mirage is costly, particularly for the many previously recognized as Métis. Many individuals who had assumed the identity of Métis and gained acceptance in that community are finding that success in achieving legal recognitition as a status Indian is accompanied by the cost of affiliation with the Métis. The Métis are saying, "If you are Indian, you cannot be a Métis." Hence, they lose whatever rights they may have attained as a result of their past or continuing affiliation with Métis communities. Of increasing concern to a growing number of persons is the fact that in Alberta, within the Métis Settlements, persons who had long been accepted as members of the Settlement communities are finding that the price they pay for recognition under the Indian Act is the cost of being stripped of their membership in the Métis Settlements. In some instances, persons in their late 80s and early 90s who founded and developed these Settlements are finding themselves and their families stripped of any land rights they may have acquired, in addition to the loss of any right to benefits or services to which their settlement membership formerly entitled them.[5] In short, they find themselves unable to enjoy the benefits of either Métis status or Indian status. This is one more aspect of the Bill C-31 question. As a result, we are seeing more communities in turmoil, division, anger, resentment, pain, and a whole lot of suffering. Where many assumed that the guarantees provided in the Charter of Rights and Freedoms in Canada would resolve and remove the inequities of discrimination, experience is instead showing that, for many Aboriginal peoples, legislation passed by both Canada and Alberta is responsible for increasing the inequities and contributing to an increasingly destructive, divisive strife within many Aboriginal communities.

There is some attempt to characterize the situation as one that arises because of a conflict between "collective" and "individual" rights. It is not at all clear that this is the case. Where an Aboriginal or treaty right has been breached or taken away by and with the authority of the Crown, the Crown has an obligation to restore that right to the individuals so deprived and it has a duty of restitution to those persons. The Crown should not be relieved of its responsibilities, nor should it be allowed to benefit illicitly from a mis-characterization of the problem for redressing the injury and providing restitution for the damages and suffering that have been and continue to be caused in its name.

Adding to our growing confusion and anger, we are beginning to see a systematic, organized, and coordinated attempt to discourage any restitution on the notion that it would represent acknowledgement of "race-based" rights, an approach rooted in an attempt to limit the notion of equality as found in the Charter of Rights and Freedoms. The Canadian Supreme Court rejected the attempt to limit the notion of "equality" in the manner now increasingly suggested by so-called theoreticians of the far right. The general approach taken seems to say that the rights of Aboriginal peoples should not be recognized because such recognition is contrary to the notion of "equality." The concept of "equality" is protected under Section 15(1) of the Charter of Rights and Freedoms: "Every individual is equal before and under the law and has the right to the equal protection and equal benefit of the law without discrimination based on race, national or ethnic origin, colour, religion, sex, age or mental or physical disability." It was generally believed that such protection would empower and protect those who had been excluded or discriminated against in the past. That general purpose of the Charter provision was recognized in the early Charter cases heard by the Supreme Court of Canada and dealt with as a way in which remedies might be provided to those so excluded or discriminated against.[6]

Aboriginal peoples first ran into the "reverse discrimination" argument in the mid-60s, prior to the enactment of the Charter of Rights and Freedoms. This approach seemed at the time to be an attempt to restrict, or, perhaps more accurately, bastardize the notion of equality as popularized by the American Civil Rights movement. We saw in the Civil Rights movement a way in which redress could be found for people discriminated against, who were being made to suffer, who were being deprived of their rights, whatever those rights were. We saw a country that was able to recognize, despite its laws and social practices, that discrimination was wrong and illegal. We saw, for the first time in our lives and in the lifetime of our parents, an example of how the concept of legal and political equality could be used as the basis upon which injustice was redressed. That debate resonated here in Canada, particularly for Aboriginal peoples, who were experiencing in the late 1960s a political reawakening.

The notion of using equality to argue for the recognition of fundamental human rights for Aboriginal people got turned on its head by the Canadian government in 1969. It decided to test a new and different notion of equality, which in essence argued that if everyone is to be recognized as equal, there should be no special status and no recognition of First Nations or Aboriginal rights in this country. It took a massive effort to stop this proposal, articulated in the so-called white paper of 1969. But that theme has recently been resurrected in Canada despite the fact that Aboriginal and treaty rights were expressly affirmed and recognized in the Canadian Constitution in 1982. The Canadian Constitution recognized both the collective and individual rights of Aboriginal peoples as an integral part of its conceptual framework underlying the notion of equality.[7]

The notion of equality as one restricted to a narrow, individual rights-based conception was purposely rejected in the way Section 15 of the Canadian Constitution was formulated. Here the political leadership appears to have attempted to extend constitutional protection by balancing the notion of collective rights and individual rights. Section 25 was introduced at the insistence of Aboriginal peoples, who sought to ensure that the notions of individual rights as recognized and protected in the Charter did not override treaty and Aboriginal rights. In some respects, we are just seeing the preliminary attempts by Canadian courts to find that balance. The wrongful acts of the Canadian nation-state, which aggressively sought to dismember First Nations and to deprive them of their fundamental rights and freedoms, cannot be allowed to use the ongoing judicial consideration of balancing collective and individual rights as a cover to avoid discharging Crown constitutional obligations. These were deliberate acts undertaken on behalf of the Crown and responsibility for equitably and fairly redressing past wrongs is neither removed or absolved by the Charter of Rights and Freedoms, nor by any terms of the Canadian Constitution.

In addition to ensuring that the Crown discharge its legal obligations and duties, Aboriginal peoples are confronted with the enormous task of nation-building or reconstruction. A large part of that effort requires that First Nations reconnect with the healing and reconciliation capabilities which are rooted in their spiritual traditions. Aboriginal peoples must recognize that the answer must be found within the cultural and traditional milieus. An increasing number of Aboriginal peoples have successfully entered the academic community and are beginning a process of connecting with Aboriginal Elders. That connection is integral to what in an academic context is called the process of deconstruction. It is a process by which Euro/Anglo and Canadian/American concepts, terms, and words are translated into an Aboriginal language and then, with the assistance of Elders, compared and analyzed. It is a challenge many Elders have welcomed and responded to with enthusiasm. It is a task well-suited to Elders for, at a conceptual level, many yearn to be involved and have the knowledge and capacity to be engaged in such a dialogue. Through this process, we try to examine the essence of the concept, and then see how it plays in our language and cultural contexts.

The deconstruction process is an essential component of our nation-building exercise. For me, this is probably one of the most rewarding kinds of exercises. I had to go through an extensive period of time training in my own language and traditions to be able to engage in that process and to identify where the comparative points are. I think that's the other thing that I find really valuable about the presentation that was made by our guest speaker. Because it seems to me that as an intellectual exercise, as an academic exercise, as a thinking exercise, we need to be able to construct a theoretical comparative framework to link the knowledge systems that are there between the First Nations and the western nations. Part of the problem in the past has been that attempts at comparative analysis have been really misguided. Past comparative exercises have been limited to attempts to find one word or one term in the English language and compare that with a corresponding term in a First Nations language. What you get from that kind of exercise is an almost total distortion of meaning, with the end result that one is unable to recognize what is being discussed. And at the end of the day you end up with an interpretation or understanding that seems to confirm the white man's worst fear of the Indian of having no conceptual capacity or understanding. Part of the problem was the fact that people who attempted such a discourse did not understand enough about the First Nations languages, traditions, and contexts that gave meaning. This is evident, for example, in many early First Nations dictionaries developed by missionaries.

What I find working with our Elders is that the Cree language and other First Nations languages organize their teachings in the form of doctrines and speak to principles. When I was active in the political community and we were going to Ottawa to make presentations to the federal government and we had our advisors and consultants and writers and they put before us stacks of paper this high for our presentation, the Elders would kind of laugh at us and tweak us at the nose and say, "How come you need so much paper to say that when all we need is a small phrase to say the same thing?" What we didn't understand then is that many of the words and phrases in our languages are really statements of general principles or doctrinal statements. The expectation was that one would look at a concept and then spend time to identify all of its subset concepts and principles. The approach inherent in this way of examining matters is not really a quaint practice unique to First Nations. The same approach is found in the study of law. The tort principle, for example, that you have a responsibility to your neighbour, stated as a doctrine of law, is a very short legal phrase, but from there you have the whole body of tort law which has evolved to apply to many different contexts. The Cree language operates in the same way.

I began my studies in the oral traditions of our people after I had grown up in the residential school system, gone through high school, and begun university. My thinking at that point had been programmed by the educational system as it then was. The Elders were concerned when I began to speak in the public forum as a political representative in this province [Alberta] that I was speaking and thinking too much like a white man. They brought me under their wing to begin teaching me and to help me begin a different process of learning. This process of learning has been ongoing for many years. At the onset of my learning experience, they said to me: Our ways are so rich. We have so much in terms of knowledge, ceremony, and process. If you are now coming home trying to find yourself and locate yourself in our conceptual world, you have to have a theoretical framework; you have to know how you measure, how you judge what you see, how you assign values, how you determine what is right, what is wrong. If you don't have that conceptual framework, the problem that you will run into is what in white language is called the "rule of man," where every man makes up his own rule, and it changes with every individual that comes along, so you're forever walking around in circles, not knowing where the hell you're coming from or where you're going. To avoid that, they said, you have to become familiar with our conceptual and theoretical framework. That was thirty years ago, and it wasn't until I was doing my graduate studies and looking at the theoretical perspectives that accompany the study of law that I got a sense of what the Elders were talking about. You can study law, and other disciplines, and go through school for four years, without being able to pull all of the component parts together, unless you are aware of a theoretical framework or perspective to apply.

In terms of our nation-building exercise, this is really our challenge today. I welcomed Sharon Venne's earlier presentation and in some ways wish I was starting law school again so I could take her class at the University of Saskatchewan. The approach she discussed represents a different paradigm from our current legal framework and the academic disciplines in this country. We need to generate a new or different analytical paradigm, not because you want to tickle someone's intellectual curiosity, but because we need to find new answers and solutions to some growing, serious problems in our communities, and in our relationships with non-Aboriginal peoples.

When we talk about treaty, for example, from a Cree perspective, we are talking about a fundamental Cree doctrine of law called *Wa-koo-towin*, the laws governing relationships. These laws establish the principles that govern the conduct and behaviour of individuals within their family environment, within their communities, and with others outside their communities. *Wa-koo-towin* provided the framework within which the treaty relationships with the Europeans were to function. It is one of the most comprehensive doctrines of law among the Cree people and contains a whole myriad of subsets of laws defining the individual and collective relationships of Cree people.

We have to be able to understand where the doctine of *Wa-koo-towin* comes from and what role it played in the treaty-making exercise. Because when our Elders lifted the pipe, when our Elders used the sweet grass, when our Elders used the ceremonies to go into a treaty-making session, they weren't putting on an anthropological show to impress Europeans newly arriving into their territory. They were doing that for a very specific reason. That was their way of moving, their way of giving life, their way of giving physical expression to the doctrine of *Wa-koo-towin*, the kind of relationship that they were under an obligation to extend to and enter into with other peoples. As Sharon mentioned, that was a practice that our peoples had for eons of time, in terms of establishing relationships with each other, with other nations. And the mutual undertaking of a relationship between the Europeans and our people, the story of that, the knowledge of that, the details of that are contained in the doctrines that the sweet grass symbolizes, that the pipe symbolizes. And our Elders tell us: If you want to understand our treaties, from our perspective, that's where you have to go to seek that knowledge. And when you have that knowledge, that will give you the definition and the description of this particular event.

What we have to do, I suppose, in putting these various concepts together, is to be able to begin placing on one side the doctrines, the philosophies, the conceptual information, to see to what extent that res- onates with our own cultural framework, our own take on what those concepts are. Because whatever concepts you find in international law, in the international community, or in the Western academic community, we have parallel extensive doctrines or concepts. The notion of human rights is not something new to our teachings; it's an integral part of our way of life as a people, rooted in what Sharon referred to as a concept of the relationship between our people and our Creator. That's where those concepts originate. What we now have to be able to do is to sit down with our Elders and look at the whole doctrine of human rights—I thought initially from the English perspective, but after listening to Patricia Seed's talk, we're going to have to bring in the Iberian perspective as well—be- cause in many ways the decolonising experience that we're going through in this country is an experience shared by peoples throughout the world. It isn't something unique to us as First Nations people. So we have to be able, like the Islamic people, or the Jews, or any other non-European nation, to look at these concepts, to see in a global framework how the various components match our own thinking, and then make them part of the institution-building that we have to be involved in as First Nation people. We have to be able to give shape, substance, and form to the governmental institutions that our people must now develop because the Canadian Constitution acknowledges our inherent sovereign rights as nations. We must also recognize that the colonial structures now in place, as defined by the Indian Act, are not structures that originate from our own people. We have to deconstruct those institutions and begin a process of reconstructing.

In a recent meeting of Elders and First Nations scholars here in Edmonton, one of the Elders raised the need to bring the hereditary system back as a system of government. The collective response of the First Nations scholars was kind of, "Oh no, not that again, it's outdated!" But when you look at that notion, both Britain and Canada have one of the oldest hereditary systems of government in the world. The concept of the Queen as the sovereign symbol of British-Canadian nations is rooted in the person of the royal occupant who isn't elected but rather is born into that position. That hereditary system of government is in place because there is a certain amount of conceptual stability associated with that form of governance. It may be that we have to revisit the concept of hereditary governance from a First Nation perspective to determine whether or not contemporary democratic institutions can be created in a manner that respects both traditional values and contemporary democratic requirements. What we need to find is a way of creating institutions that have stability, cohesion, and relevance. What the Elders speak about is really the wish of any organized nation or society: a governance system and institutions that reflect our own values and traditions.

The analytic or conceptual approach I have described is integral to our process of nation building. It is also a necessary component of the healing and reconciliation process that needs to happen in Indian country if we are meaningfully to address issues dealing with identity and finding solutions to repair the damage and injury wrought upon and suffered by too many individuals. I really appreciated the opportunity to listen in to the conversations and presentations made today because I usually judge the value of a meeting by how much I learn from it, rather than hearing the same old stuff all over again, perhaps repeated in different fashions. With all of the presentations I really learned a lot, and I again thank the organizers for the opportunity and privilege of learning with you today.

1 Editor's note: Dr. Cardinal revised the text of his talk on three occasions before his illness prevented him from further work. Beyond correcting a few minor typos and incorrect bibliographic references, I haven't altered this version since it represents the last sense he gave me before passing of how he wanted his original talk to appear in print. For more information on the editing process, see the Introduction.

2 I use the term "white community" in the way the Supreme Court of Canada has approached the term "word of the white man." In R. v. Sioui (1990), the Supreme Court of Canada stated that the term "treaty" was not a term of art, but a formal word identifying agreements in which the "word of the white man" is given by European/ Canadian representatives to make certain of the "Indians' co-operation" (S.C.R. 1025, para. 44). I use the term "white community" as a term of art to describe Anglo/American and French/Canadian approaches to First Nations peoples.

3 According to the Indian Act R.S.C. 1985 c. I-5 s. 2(1), an "Indian" is a person who is "pursuant to this Act and is registered as an Indian or is entitled to be registered as an Indian."

4 See St. Catherine's Milling and Lumber Co. v. The Queen (1888).

5 According to the Metis Settlement Act R.S.A 2000, CM-14 s. 90(1), "a settlement member terminates membership in a settlement if (a) the person voluntarily becomes registered as an Indian under the Indian Act (Canada)."

6 See, for example, Andrews v. Law Society of British Columbia (1989) 1. S.C.R. 143. Since then, the Supreme Court has heard many cases dealing with varying aspects of S.15(1), giving rise to continuing concerns by many.

7 See the Charter of Rights and Freedoms, s. 15(1); Sections 35 and 25.

QUESTIONS & DISCUSSION

PARTICIPANT: The tracing of the difference in treaties and different linguistic traditions interests me. My question is for Patricia Seed: Is there something else happening in those traditions that determines that difference? Why is it that the English treaty process develops in that way, other than the history of the word, and the Portuguese and Spanish traditions developed in a different direction? Is there an underlying social-economic process that's involved, and how would you begin to unpack those differences?

PATRICIA SEED: I suspect they introduced the requirement for a written document in acquiring land from the natives because of unresolved and irresolvable conflicts among English colonists in the New World over land boundaries. Often there were multiple purchasers for a single area in the New World and all of the purchasers relied upon verbal agreements. A great many English purchasers with multiple verbal agreements very quickly became a major headache for political leaders in the New World. Unwilling or unable to use native understandings of ownership or use rights to decide who had the greater right to the land, colonial leaders were unable to settle these conflicts. Colonists doggedly continued to fight each other over property ownership. These and similar conflicts pushed the adoption of the mandatory written document to transfer land in England in 1682 and then, of course, in the colonies as well. This statute allowed English officials a legal way for deciding conflicts among the colonists about land boundaries.

This leads to a second issue: what does the word "purchase" mean in English? What it means is that you turn something over to somebody else permanently, in exchange for what the English language calls a *valuable* consideration. But that doesn't answer the question of what's valuable; whose standard of value are you using? Furthermore, the word "purchase" contains the notion of permanent alienability. In other words, that I can give this money to the person next to me, and she maybe lends me a pen. But that doesn't mean that I have purchased it, for I might have merely rented it for a time. English settlers assumed that in any transaction in which they gave Aboriginal people something that they thought was valuable in exchange for land, the swap was permanent.

Another peculiar dimension of English land law is the confusion of the right to own with actual physical possession. You know the sixteenth-century saying that possession is eleven points of the law, which then becomes "possession is nine tenths of the law." In other words, "if I have land, it's mine." In most western European legal systems, this is a very bizarre notion because it's the person who has the legal title that has a right to it, and not the person who actually physically possesses it.

PARTICIPANT: Patricia talked about the difference in New Zealand, which is also part of the same English tradition. I wondered whether there's anything more than the simple fact that there was a dual language version. This is an important reality because, as Sharon Venne made clear, the language of the other side never gets articulated much in Canada and doesn't enter into the debate. Ours is a largely settler discourse. Unless you seek out an alternative, it's very hard to hear the other side. But I'm wondering if there are other factors.

PATRICIA SEED: You mean in the contemporary situation in New Zealand? There is something else. When Britain decided to join the common market in 1971, they basically jettisoned all of the economic supports that they had for the purchase of things like land and butter from both New Zealand and Australia. Since Britain had rejected them in favor of their fellow Europeans, I think that a lot of *Pakeha* (English New Zealanders) and Australians decided that Britain had abandoned them and that they were going to find some kind of Aboriginal or Native heritage as part of *their* rebuilding of their own image of themselves. So it became part of what I think of as the postcolonial national imaginaries of both Australia and New Zealand. In New Zealand what they've done has been remarkable; they've reintroduced Maori in the schools, including in the Pakeha schools, so that Pakeha now grow up knowing at least some Maori. They've really made a change to a deliberate kind of bicultural society.

That is not to say that everyone is happy with the present situations. There is a tension there and I don't want to deny it. You can find plenty of people in New Zealand who are hostile to Maori gains. Sometimes I hear resentments over the size of large settlements. Many Pakeha ask why the Wharangei River dwellers (a large North Island community) received such a large share of land. Despite the underlying resentment, on the surface of these exchanges there's a sense that, yes, the Maori were here first; this was their territory; we did come to it; and we have to figure out some kind of accommodation.

PARTICIPANT: Sharon, can you talk a bit more about the spirit and the intent of the treaties from an Indigenous perspective? What things were understood by the treaties, over and above the things that were written down in the text? I find that really fascinating in terms of what I've been hearing here. What was understood to be part of the treaty besides just the written components of it?

SHARON VENNE: One of the really critical things about the treaties that I did not touch on relates to treaties under international law. Article three of the Vienna Convention on Treaties recognizes that the written version and the oral version of a Treaty are at the same level: they are equal under international law. What does that mean? It means that one version does not dominate the other version. There is a very spiritual reason related to the Cree legal system. When the Elders talk about the spirit in the intent of the Treaty, what is it really? At the time of the making of the Treaty, what was in the minds of the people on both sides when they were at the table? What were they agreeing on? It is that agreement embodied in the oral understanding of the Treaty from the Elders' perspective. In reality, the oral understanding of the Treaty is more legitimate than the non-Indigenous written version, but I do not want to get into a big discussion about Cree law at this time. Let me just conclude by saying that the actual meaning of the spirit of the treaty-making relates to the Cree legal system and the relationship between the Cree people and the Creation. It is the working of our own legal system, our own Cree legal system and what they were doing at the time of the treaty-making and who was the witness at the time of the treaty-making. Who were the witnesses besides the treaty commissioner and the Elders? The Creation witnessed the two sides sitting, talking, and agreeing. Indigenous Peoples always know that there was a witness to that process. The witness was the Creation—or the spirit of the treaty, if I can put it in those words. Regardless of the

Crown's writings, there will always be the Creation who will make the corrections.

PARTICIPANT: Sharon, you mentioned a book you had written.

SHARON VENNE: My book, *Our Elders Understand Our Rights*, is about the history of Indigenous Peoples at the United Nations. It recounts some of the struggle to move an international community from looking at us as objects to seeing us as subjects. Even now, most people, even representatives of Canada at the United Nations, talk about us as "our Indians," as if we belong to them, which I find very offensive. I don't belong to anybody. I belong to my own person; I belong to my own nation. We're trying to move the thinking of people from seeing us as objects to seeing that we are subjects of international law, that, as a nation, we have the right to make decisions about our own people, our own future. It's a big step for them to take, because I think that the colonizers are addicted to us. I'm working on a twelve-step program actually about how to break the colonizer's addiction. The first step is that they have to admit that they are powerless over us. I joke about it, but it's a serious thing for people to break that hold they try to have on us. It is like an addiction, you know; they can't seem to let us go to be our own persons. The book is about that.

PARTICIPANT: Sharon, could you follow up on the international tribunal that's being formed at the United Nations?

SHARON VENNE: This is something that Indigenous Peoples are working on. What we have been talking about at the United Nations, the model we've been using, is the model that the United Nations had on the subject of apartheid during the apartheid regime in South Africa. People that were violating the resolutions related to apartheid went on these lists of people where you should not shop in their stores. There was a boycott of their goods and services. Countries who were trading with South Africa, these countries were treated differently at the United Nations. It is a model that can be used by Indigenous Peoples who have their Treaty rights violated by the state governments. The rights of Indigenous Peoples could form part of a report to the general assembly on a yearly basis. These reports could list the countries violating the rights of Indigenous Peoples, the Treaty violators. How do you get those countries to comply with the treaties? One of the biggest things that goes on at the international level is the shaming. I mean, I don't know if Canadians can be shamed. I haven't quite figured out if they can or cannot. But how can you make a state comply with the treaties? Of course, countries like Canada, the United States, New Zealand, and others are very much against external reviews of Treaty violations. Canada is quite quick to say that they're working on an internal process to deal with Treaty violations. The trouble with that is it's set up under parliament. They control it. If you don't agree with the government then they take the funding away, or they put people in there who only follow the government policy. So there are a lot of problems with it internally. Of course, we're going to have some of those problems externally, too, if Canada has its own people sitting on the board, but these issues can be worked on and developed in the future.

PARTICIPANT: Pat, would you please talk more about the construction of the native as "hunter"?

PATRICIA SEED: The colonial fiction in the English-speaking world was the hunter. And, in fact, the reason the "hunter" has to do with Native Americans (and I go into this in my book, *American Pentimento*) has a very complicated history in terms of English law and Norman law about the kinds of rights hunters had. In this tradition, hunters weren't people who actually could own the land because hunting rights were separable from land rights. And so a hunter was somebody who didn't have, under English law, the right to own the land. So we have the debates over the creation of this fiction of the not-quite-human person. But the fiction is created wholly in terms of Anglo-Saxon and in particular Anglo-Norman law. So this notion supports the idea that the natives don't cultivate the land. One of the things that I do in the book is I have maps, and I do quite a lot with maps, but I have maps of sedentary cultivators—there are cultivators all over the place. In fact, there are sedentary cultivators—what are the Cherokee doing when they get pushed out of Georgia in the 1830s? They're cotton farmers. These people are growing cotton on huge plantations. These are not hunters, but the colonial fiction of not-quite-human somehow overrides the reality. So, this whole question of cultivation, purchase, and treaty are the three fictions by which Englishmen propose that they own the New World. The Spaniards and Portuguese have different fictions, and they're equally fictionalized, but they're all equally inventive and real and used in their own system—it's just not land, that's all.

SHARON VENNE: Look at the debates during the time of Columbus. They decided that we were human beings, but not equal to European human beings because we weren't Christianized. The Papal Bull of 1493 said that we couldn't own our own land because we weren't Christian and that they could use all force to convert us to Christianity and that if they kill us in the conversion process, so be it. That Papal Bull is still on the books, still part of the Catholic church, still the bedrock of the Catholic faith. In 1992, Indigenous Peoples at the United Nations at the Working Group on Indigenous Peoples wrote a letter to the Pope to ask if, as a show of good faith to Indigenous Peoples, he could rescind this Papal Bull and recognize us as human beings capable of owning our land. We wrote up this letter, signed it "Indigenous Peoples from around the world," and sent it to Pope John Paul II. About six or seven months later, we got a letter back from him, saying, no, he couldn't rescind the Papal Bull because the Catholic church was still celebrating evangelism in the Americas and around the world. 1992 was the celebration of five hundred years of evangelism in the Americas, and he would not rescind that Papal Bull that said that we cannot own our lands because we're not Christian. This example underlines the whole of Western thought in the Americas that, from a Christian point of view, we are not human beings and that, because we're not human beings like all other human beings, then we can be treated like this cup; if this cup is getting in your way, you move it. And that's how people still look at us. Governments look at us like that. Average Canadian citizens still think that if we're in their way, we should be removed. This thinking is really deeply embedded in the psyche of Christianity. Celebrating five hundred years of evangelism in the Americas, to me, is not a celebration. And I'm not discounting any Christians in the room, but I think there has to be some thought put into this whole idea.

PARTICIPANT: What's your view of the modern treaties? Do they represent a step forward from the kinds of situations you're describing?

SHARON VENNE: There's no such thing as a modern treaty. You either have a treaty or you don't have a treaty. Canada tried to perpetuate this idea that they're entering into modern treaties, when actually what they're doing is domesticating themselves and coming under the jurisdiction of the state of Canada. Recently, I've been in the North listening to the chiefs of the so-called new Treaty areas talking about what's happened to them. And what's happened is that their territories have been taken over, and so their relationship with the land is no longer there and they can't make decisions in relation to the land, which is contrary to what they had been told in the agreements. Canada has been pushing this idea that if you're going to make an agreement with them, then your rights to the land are extinguished. I always say that *if* the original treaties were to read "people surrender their land," then why would they need an extinguishment clause? The only reason you need an extinguishment clause is that Indigenous Peoples obviously never gave up anything at the time of the treaty-making. Why would you extinguish something you already extinguished? That would be a legal nullity. So now they've changed the word because they've been under such criticism internationally for use of the word "extinguishment." Now Canada uses a new word, "certainty," and to me this is the same as "extinguish." It doesn't matter how you cut it, they're still pushing that they want now for Indigenous Peoples to give up our relationship with the land completely and then to turn it over to the state of Canada. The only thing that can help at an international tribunal dealing with this whole issue is acknowledgment of the fact that the Elders and the people who completed the agreement did not give their fully informed consent because they didn't know the nature of the agreement. Now it's coming out that the Elders and the chiefs are saying, "That's not what we agreed to," that they never gave their consent to what Canada was pushing on them.

PARTICIPANT: What about modern treaties like the Nisga'a Agreement?

SHARON VENNE: I don't consider the Nisga'a Agreement to be a treaty because the three parties that were making this agreement are Canada, the Nisga'a, and the province of British Columbia. The province of British Columbia does not have any international treaty-making capacity. In the process of the Nisga'a Agreement there is no modern treaty. It is a big hoax because British Columbia does not have treaty-making capacity. If there had been an agreement between Canada and the Nisga'a, then *that* could be considered a treaty. The agreement with Nunavut is a treaty. It was made between the Inuit and Canada. When you throw British Columbia into the mix you are just making another agreement. In the future, if the Nisga'a come to the United Nations for assistance with their agreement, they might argue that they made this agreement with British Columbia and Canada. The United Nations would have to say that the Nisga'a were not in the Treaty protected by international law nor is the Nisga'a Agreement subject to the rules of interpretation and implementation at the UN. Canada is perpetuating the idea of a modern treaty, but if you look at Dr. Martinez's study, the UN will say that it's not a modern treaty. It's a constructive arrangement between people, but it is not a treaty within the international legal system.

PARTICIPANT: Sharon was talking about hopefully changing perceptions of Indigenous people in Canada. I'm wondering if there is a Cree equivalent to the Maori word for *Pakeha*? From what I know of New Zealand culture, in the usage of the term *Pakeha* there is an implicit understanding of the white culture's foreignness from the land. I'm wondering if there's a Cree equivalent that you would suggest or promote?

SHARON VENNE: In Cree we call foreigners *wapiskusuki.* Of course, in any Indigenous language, there is always a word for people who do not belong. Now, I don't know whether the non-Indigenous people would want to use the term or not.

PARTICIPANT: Also, in terms of the way that Canadians tend to contextualize our position as French Canadian, Czech-Canadian, Dutch-Canadian, or whatever our descendants. There seems to be this trouble with positioning ourselves as colonizers or settlers, because we've been here for x generations. So I was thinking that an Indigenous name, like the Maori word *Pakeha*, would be an effective way for non-Native people to identify themselves.

SHARON VENNE: To me, it doesn't matter how long the colonizers live in our land, they'll always be colonizers. The number of generations doesn't diminish the fact that they're still living here under the sufferance of the Treaty peoples. I think that people who are living here under Treaty have to understand what their Treaty rights are and to understand that there are limitations on what those rights are. Because right now people don't know the limitations placed on them by the treaty process and they think that they can go anywhere and do anything on our land without respecting the land and resources. It's very critical, especially now because of all the pollution and destruction of the resources, that there be a real attempt by the non-Indigenous peoples to understand what their Treaty limitations are. You're not children, so quit acting like spoiled children in our land because it's not acceptable, and it's not really respectful of the Treaty position that your ancestors asked our ancestors to live under. I keep telling non-Indigenous peoples to grow up and take responsibility for the Treaty because that's what you're living here under. And understand that and live that, because we do. We respect non-Indigenous people who know they're living in our lands; we know that they're here for a reason, and we try to respect it even though sometimes you just grind your teeth and you want to duke it out with a few people. We try to follow the Elders' understanding. It tries our patience, you know, but we try to be respectful.

HAROLD CARDINAL: With respect to the last question, I guess it depends on whether you want to be a polite Cree in terms of the name. But in our tradition, in our way as Cree people, we have a name or designation for all visitors, *Omantiw*. This seems to me a very appropriate description of all the people who are not native to our land. I had one quick comment I wanted to make and then two questions, and I suppose the first is a quasi-question as well. We went over very briefly the non-human undercurrent to the colonial discourse, and in some ways in Canada that's typical of academics: they're uncomfortable discussing a racist theory that tries to legitimize the claim to ownership of the First Nation territories. In Canada, such theories have encouraged a deeply embedded form of institutional racism which in turn informs the values taught in our educational system. So deeply embedded are these racist doctrines that people don't know that they are getting shoved into their psyches and that they're spouting it out. This is one of the continuing examples of the kind of role that the Roman Catholic Church played and it's not well known amongst the general population.

The other racist doctrine is the doctrine of discovery, the notion of *terra nullius* here in Canada. Again, I think that you still can go through university, and, unless you happen to bump into a Native professor somewhere, you can go through five, six years, even ten years of university in Canada without ever having to deal with or confront the notion of the doctrine of discovery. That is a legal doctrine adopted by the Supreme Court of Canada on a continuing basis—that is a package that hasn't been dealt with.

My question [to Patricia Seed] is: how do you encourage academics to confront directly the very racist doctrines that underpin some of the most important institutions in this country? For example, in Canadian law, when dealing with any matter to do with First Nations rights, particularly the right of land, we have first to defeat what I call the presumption of savagery. We have to prove in court that our nations were not primitive, or that they had a basic semblance of organizational form to them, in order to enable the court to be able to proceed. The second question is more getting a sense of your comparative study between New Zealand, American, and Canadian treaty-making. In the US, treaty-making stopped some time in the 1800s. Where is New Zealand in terms of how they view whether treaty was a once-and-for-all?

PATRICIA SEED: It was once-and-for-all. It was 1840—that was it.

HAROLD CARDINAL: In that context, I wanted your thoughts on the neo-treaty-making approach that Canada is putting forward. That was the third element of my question.

PATRICIA SEED: How do you fight the presumption of sub-humanity or non-humanity? That's a very tough one. You're right: it's engrained in the schools, popular culture, art, literature. There are lots of fronts on which this notion is perpetrated. I think that one of the reasons why people in post-colonial English societies, such as Canada, the United States, New Zealand, and Australia, become attached to these myths—and this is very distinctive of our societies—is that there's a desire to somehow differentiate our post-colonial society from England.

Some people in these nations are creating an English post-colonial society by making use of—it's kind of a cultural property borrowing—something of Aboriginal people. Now, I know some people have suggested using contemporary intellectual property rights. The argument goes like this: If you want to borrow something of ours, you have to ask our permission first. That's one strategy. My strategy in *American Pentimento* is to put everybody's notion of sub-humanity into the same category, using a comparative approach. Because one of the things that I'm constantly running into is, yes, the statement of "our Indians," which always appalled me. People are always saying that "our Indians" are treated better than, say, in the English system, or the Portuguese, or in Brazil. So I put everybody on the same level, and I do it comparatively, and I show you how different people are doing the same kinds of things. Sometimes it's the old biblical thing about it being easier to recognize the speck in your neighbour's eye. I'm hoping that by recognizing the speck in their neighbour's eye, they can recognize the speck in their own. That's my strategy in *American Pentimento* for fighting these assumptions.

Comparative thinking always shifts around, depending upon the place from which you start. Take recent Canadian treaty-making—Nisga'a and Nunavut. On the one hand, Nunavut is wonderful if you're in the United States and you want to talk about why we couldn't have Cherokee government in Oklahoma, when in fact Oklahoma was going to be a Native American state before the United States government decided that we couldn't have an indigenous state. And so, teaching in a US classroom, I can say, well, you've got Nunavut, which is a Native-run state. What's wrong with having a Native-run state? It works very well in that critical comparative kind of context, but of course the problem for the inhabitants of Nunavut has been the tradeoff, the lack of access to petroleum income and the opening up of the northwest area of the country for oil and mineral exploration. Both are real downsides of political independence. What I understand is that the leaders of Nunavut were politically savvy enough to realize that that was the only way that they could get some kind of self-government. Those options were unavailable to natives in Oklahoma during the last century.

PARTICIPANT: I was wondering under what grounds Native peoples have been able to stop or minimize oil and gas development in areas where they don't want it?

PATRICIA SEED: Ecuador's been one of the more interesting cases because Texaco absolutely devastated the landscape and peoples. Two communities in Ecuador, the Cofan and Secoya, are near the brink of extinction because of the diseases that Texaco brought. When these communities went to the national government and the national congress to complain, there was dead silence. The strategy they devised, which I think is brilliant, is to sue Texaco to recover the damages done to their community. They challenged Texaco in White Plains, New York (its headquarters), but the damage had already been done. In other words, all that they could sue for is some kind of restitution.[1]

Aboriginal peoples in Spanish and Portuguese America do not have any potential of calling upon a national, political, or cultural understanding to stop mining, particularly petroleum mining. That is too touchy an issue; petroleum is seen as a state-owned resource and, as such, must be managed by the state, by the national government, just the way it's managed by the Spanish Crown in the colonial era. It's one of those political hot buttons that you can really touch. I mean, the North American oil companies never really understood it. In 1934, Standard Oil didn't understand, and got kicked out of Bolivia and Mexico. Texaco used to be the Texas and Mexican gas company; it's now just the Texas Company (Texaco). The nationalizations were immensely politically popular! One of the ways that you can really rally a political assembly any place in Spanish America is to talk about petroleum. So, Aboriginal peoples' rights to petroleum are very tricky. I don't advise making that a national issue in any of the Iberian colonies, particularly the Spanish American colonies.

In Brazil, it's complicated because during the military dictatorship, which began in 1964 but really came down with a heavy hand in 1967, what you had was an opportunity for political dissent by discussing the Aboriginal people of the Amazon. Thus the military only allowed political dissent to be expressed regarding Aboriginal peoples in the Amazon and the extent of Indigenous rights to the gold in the region. Thus, although there are many debates that you can read from the 1970s and the 1980s supposedly about Aboriginal peoples in the Amazon, you have to decode them first. In other words, you have to reinterpret what was said in terms of the political discourse that was going on about the left and the right and the military in Brazil because sometimes, and very often, Aboriginal peoples are meant to stand for the position of certain political parties within Brazil. You can't read those debates openly. In other words, they're not transparent statements about the Aboriginal peoples from the '70s and '80s.

During that repressive time, however, the military actually wound up being a quasi-protector, for a very brief period, of Aboriginal peoples. But this was while they were disappearing hundreds of left-wing people. Thus you had a government half-heartedly protecting indigenous people while murdering political opponents.

As soon as the military resigned and the democratically elected government took over, the military reverted to its traditional position, which is basically covert support for the far right-wing landowners in Brazil who have a devious strategy for invading aboriginal territory.

What you see portrayed in the American press is only partly true. I don't read Canadian press on Brazilian Indians, so I don't know what has come across there, but in the US press the invasion of indigenous regions is portrayed as the competition between two groups of very poor people, between the Yanomami, for example, and the landless peasants of the northeast. What the papers don't mention is that, in fact, the landless peasants are very often backed by the major right-wing landowners who want to get rid of the native people by introducing all kinds of diseases. And so you have the replication of the kinds of practices that occurred in the United States—deliberate introduction of malaria and smallpox blankets, all the kinds of horrible biological warfare that people like to deny happen, but in fact happen.

In Brazil, there is an appeal that you can use on behalf of Indigenous people, which is to appeal basically to groups of northern European NGO (non-governmental organizations) conservationists. Many of these are Scandinavian-based and, having destroyed all of their own forests, want to preserve the Amazon rainforest. So you can bring, actually, a lot of international pressure to bear on the Brazilian government by calling upon these largely northern Europeans and sometimes US environmental groups to lobby—but you don't have that option in Spanish America.

PARTICIPANT: This is a question about the role of academics in relation to imperialism. I'm sure you [Patricia Seed] and Sharon Venne are familiar with the Hawaiian example where the Hawaiian people tried to argue that sacred sites are being bombed by the US military, and an anthropologist published a paper indicating that these sacred sites were not from time immemorial—they were fairly recent, as a kind of reconstructive cultural movement. That paper was used by the US government to justify demolishing these sacred sites. That is a pretty shocking example of how academics can be used to justify such actions. How do you see that?

PATRICIA SEED: I have a position on this. An incredible kind of hypocrisy exists in the English language tradition and it goes back to a seventeenth-century English mythification of the New World. There's a statement from John Locke which I *love* to hate: "In the beginning, all the world was America." What do you mean, "in the beginning"? America is America now. America isn't the way England was twenty, thirty years ago, or a hundred years ago, but that's what he meant. He meant that the Native peoples of the Americas had what he thought was a form of communal land ownership that, in England, was being displaced by large landowners grabbing land, claiming it for themselves, and kicking out all the smallholders—all the communal holders, all the collective holders. So, what he does is constitute America as the imagined past of England, a kind of mythical period of English history. This moment, and this movement, does not occur in *any* Iberian language literature on the New World. Why? Because they're not undergoing the same economic transformation—they're not moving from communal land to large individual properties. Rather, they've got a collection, as they've always had, of communal, collective, and corporately held (in a pre-corporate kind of sense) communities—they all exist at the same time. So they don't have this notion that there is a *past*, and they don't try to reinvent the Americas as the past that they once had.

This creates an immense hypocrisy—that Aboriginal peoples *must* prove that what they did was what they did in time immemorial. Why? Why can't they change? Do you want to tell the settler community that they can only build houses the way they used to on the plains here? When did these people own the present? Why does a Hawaiian community have to prove that it belongs to time immemorial? They've made it a sacred site—it's their sacred site! Why can't they change? Why does what they do have to belong to this timeless, eternal, prehistorical past? Why can't they fish with new instruments? Why can't they use contemporary technology? The settlers do. It's part of this distinction that tries, and succeeds a lot of the time, to permanently keep Aboriginal peoples on the other side—and that is to say, they don't belong to history. History begins with the coming of the people with writing, the people of the book. In *American Pentimento*, I'm actually very critical of the way people in New Zealand use Alan Henson's piece—Alan Henson talked about how certain Maori customs were in fact created. Well, in the light of the colonial present, of course! What culture doesn't interact with other cultures around it, and recreate itself in terms of changing circumstances? Why is it that that becomes politically such a powerful issue? Everybody has a right to belong to the present if they want to. Everybody has a right to make technological change if they want to. So, I find that whole premise to be a very questionable one, and it's what people make of that story that I wind up calling into question.

PARTICIPANT: My question relates to what you [Patricia Seed] were saying about the Iberian tradition being a different one. Of course, from the sixteenth-century point of view, the Black Legend that the Spaniards were the ones actively killing and displacing Aboriginal peoples helped other European nations to differentiate their brand of colonialism. What role if any does the Black Legend play in the Iberian traditions you were discussing?

PATRICIA SEED: The Black Legend originated in an internal critique of Spanish colonization. The Spanish insisted that all native peoples be Christianized. As a native you didn't have an option to keep your faith, to keep your spiritual connections to the past—that was not ever an issue to the Spanish colonists. The difficult issue for the Spaniards was *how* were they going to Christianize the natives?

The western Christian tradition is torn—divided—between the peaceful means and the military means of conversion. And so the constant tension in the Spanish empire centred on *how* are we going to Christianize? Are we going to take the sword, like Charlemagne did, and say, Convert, or I'll cut your head off? Or, are we going to have a dialogue (that means we're going to talk to you), and after a while you're going to become Christian. The end result is the same—mandatory Christianization.

Bartholomé de Las Casas argued within this tradition for the peaceful means of conversion and, as a result, he developed this very powerful negative critique of the military tradition, which he identified as Islamic. Las Casas sought to prevent conquerors from launching a military attack immediately after reading the requirement. He wanted to provide a long interval of gradual conversion.

I wrote about this critique in *Ceremonies of Possession* in a chapter on the requirement, which is how the Spanish legally take possession. Spaniards take legal possession of the New World by reading a text, because they possess bodies and not land. A nineteenth-century French writer calls it the conquest of souls, but it's not quite right because to sixteenth-century Spaniards an Indian soul wasn't quite human—it's slightly anachronistic to use "conquest of souls." It would be better to say that when Spaniards read a text they were conquering bodies.

But when England began to have the technological capacity to challenge Spain in the Atlantic at the end of the sixteenth century, they began to develop their own rationales for displacing Spanish rule. They turned to Las Casas's critique of the Spanish military tradition of forcing conversion and therefore political rule. The English competitors, however, said, Oh, look at the Spanish, look at all of these horrible atrocities! And they *are* horrible: I've never been able to teach Las Casas because I find it too despicable. It's beyond human understanding how horrible it is.

But the English colonizers did not take Las Casas's observations as a critique of any use of force against indigenous people. Nor did they take it as the means to effect Christianization of the Americas. Rather, the English used this critique in a very political kind of way only to dismiss the Spanish. And that is the origin of the Black Legend.

The Black Legend appalls me because its core message opposes the use of force against aboriginal peoples. Yet while criticizing Spaniards for military actions, English colonizers fail even to admit responsibility for their own killing of aboriginal peoples.

Several years ago I read the narratives that the French, the Dutch, and the English had written about wars with the Mohegans. The Dutch have a very pacifist tradition, so they were very divided, and some questioned whether it was right to fight native peoples under any circumstances. Some Dutch settlers said yes, others said no, so there was a tension that allowed critical perspectives and debate over the legitimacy of military action. Unlike the Dutch, French colonists in New York did not publicly debate the legitimacy of military action against natives. Rather, French colonizers occasionally expressed regret for tactical mistakes—you know, you really shouldn't have done that. There wasn't quite the same regret that there was with killing a Frenchman, but, on the other hand, some French colonists thought that maybe this killing isn't such a shrewd policy. But from the English—there's silence. The Pequot massacre—I mean, they're killing women and children and they're writing about the screams of the dying in a triumphalist fashion. And there's *no* discussion afterwards—there's just this kind of heavy silence from 1634 up until King Phillip's war. So, on the one hand, I don't want to justify what the Spaniards did because I can't deal with it, but on the other hand, it really bothers me that there isn't this tradition of criticism and regret and apology for the killings not far from here. It puzzles me. I want to spend some time in the future thinking about why there isn't this kind of critical tradition—and when can you start to criticize the tradition and the killings of native people, and when are you absolutely politically prohibited from doing so.

PARTICIPANT: Harold, you shared with us that you had been through the European academic system. How could post-secondary institutions do a better job of providing Aboriginal students with that cultural fit?

HAROLD CARDINAL: One of the models that I've seen that has worked and is working is a kind of partnering that you find in Saskatchewan between the Saskatchewan Indian Federated College [now the First Nations University of Canada] and the Universities of Saskatchewan and Regina. Similar arrangements exist between the Gabriel Dumont Institute and the same universities. There one sees formal partnerships between First Nations- and Aboriginal-controlled institutions on one hand and the Universities of Saskatchewan and Regina on the other. Such an arrangement has enabled the SIFC to grant degrees through the University of Regina. These are useful working models.

But we have a real problem in our academic institutions that needs to be addressed and overcome, I think. Even though the Supreme Court decision in Delgamuukw (1997) legitimized the information from oral traditions and accorded oral traditions the same weight as written sources, the perception still remains that written documents are superior, more accurate and reliable, and therefore to be trusted more than information from oral traditions.

This misperception arises from the fact that, even though the white man has been amongst our people for over five hundred years, he still knows little about First Nations people. There is a general ignorance of the fact that First Nations have imposed really tough discipline on the way in which certain kinds of information is to be transmitted or passed on. In many First Nations there are strict laws, rules, and regulations governing how certain information or knowledge is transmitted from one person to another, from one generation to another. Part of the difficulty is that all that has been seen is the verbal transmission of the information. What hasn't been seen or understood are the stringent laws our nations have developed through centuries, laws enabling us to judge the validity and accuracy of information. If we were to do a comparative analysis, I would think, quite easily, that our laws and regulations are far more stringent than anything in Western academia, in terms of the standards that would have to be met by information, but we haven't done this kind of analysis.

In the meantime, we need to generate the kind of academic exercise to provide comfort to those who require it, not only sceptical white people but also, more importantly, Aboriginal peoples in our respective communities. We need to know that the information we're dealing with is something we can trust and rely on. So we have to be able to identify and explain those things and make sure that the information that we deal with, in either system of knowledge, is one that is reliable in the long run. Once we do that perhaps we can allay some of the concerns that those coming from written traditions have about the information and the systems in the oral traditions. That's at one level. I don't think, for example, that even where we have partnered institutions the process has begun to address that. Sometimes I think we become too defensive when we look at these kinds of issues instead of trying to deal with what it is that we have to overcome—and hopefully that kind of process can occur sooner rather than later.

We also have a warped notion of what Elders or knowledge keepers are in the western tradition, and we often undervalue them. We ask an Elder to our meeting and if [he or she] opens the meeting with a prayer and then shuts up for the rest of the meeting and closes it off again, we think we're using the Elders the way we should. We don't acknowledge that, in a professional sense, they have spent a lifetime studying a particular subject matter; they are no different than the PhD students who've spent their academic lives focusing on a particular area of study. We have to be able to give contemporary acknowledgment to the kind of knowledge that Elders have—particularly in educational institutions (because you asked in a university context).

One of the most refreshing experiences I had as a student was taking a comparative law course at Tel Aviv University in Israel. The course examined the legal systems of the United States, the State of Israel, and traditional Jewish law. We had an American judge to talk about the criminal procedures in the American legal system, an Israeli law professor who dealt with the State Criminal laws of Israel, and a Jewish Rabbi who presented the approaches used by traditional Jewish law. In that team teaching approach, there was absolutely no question that the Rabbi had as much legitimate information to impart as the American judge and Israeli law professor.

We need to find similar ways to recognize our knowledge keepers and accord them the same kind of respect that ought to be theirs in the academic community. This old idea of the academic running to the Elders to get information and then turning around and being the recognized white expert has to end soon. If we're going to continue the tradition of enabling our knowledge keepers to grow and address the future needs of our people, we need to have a system in place that recognizes and values their contributions. Such an approach will provide many young people, and maybe many of the middle generation, validation and reaffirmation. Such an approach would signal to our Elders that their knowledge is viewed by others as valuable and relevant. They need to know that.

PARTICIPANT: Frank Tough, if they did find that, because of the scrip fraud, Aboriginal title wasn't surrendered properly, what would be the consequences?

FRANK TOUGH: Well, I'm not sure that fraud in scrip will defeat the Crown's argument that there was a clear and plain intent to extinguish, but if (and I'm not a lawyer) the courts decided that Aboriginal title was breached, then that would set off the process of negotiations. So a possible outcome of that would be some form of new land tenure for the Métis, some compensation.

PATRICIA SEED: Was there any attempt to adopt a Torrens land system in Canada?[2] They did that in several other colonies. Did they consider it here?

FRANK TOUGH: Yes, in western Canada in 1869–70, in an area attached to the Dominion. They set up a survey system that's not unlike the American system in the West, in terms of townships and ranges, and there is a system of land registry. But it's jurisdictionally a little more complicated because the province of Manitoba, for example, was a self-governing entity that did not have ownership or management over the lands. And because it was in the process of being surveyed and settled, there wasn't a system of municipalities either. So, through a process of fee simple patents, they issued patents to the land that were then registered as a local title. But I think it was intended to implement a Torrens system.

PARTICIPANT: [Question inaudible.]

FRANK TOUGH: Well, it's an interesting problem because the federal courts are looking to an Aboriginal practice as something that is integral to the culture before contact with Europeans. We know that the Métis are defined as an Aboriginal people, but they're also the consequence of contact with the European.[3] In about 1778, Peter Pond goes up into the Lake Athabasca country, and the North West Company follows from there.[4] And with the North West Company and the Hudson's Bay Company in that area you get the genesis of a Métis population.

PARTICIPANT: Frank, I was curious, to what extent are there oral narratives that support your archival research?

FRANK TOUGH: There is a bit. The other thing that I came across—and in fact the trial judge asked me about this—is that some of the Elders said that the Church had taken their scrip coupons and certificates. We have written documents that prove that the Church was involved with taking possession of the coupons and that they were in cahoots with Revillon Frères.[5] So there's a few bits. But what I would say about most of this stuff is that in a way it's an archive—they don't know what the state of their application is; they have no idea of this process.

NOTES

1 Seed: This is the first lawsuit filed in the U.S. by foreign plaintiffs alleging environmental damage overseas. The US judge gave Texaco a choice of a U.S. or Ecuadorian trial; they opted for the latter.
2 Tough: A system of land registration, devised by Sir Richard Robert Torrens, based on a description of every land parcel, name of the owner, and anyone else who had an interest in the parcel of land.
3 Tough: The question of whether or not the Métis have Aboriginal rights, notwithstanding the fact that they are a result of contact, was decided by the Supreme Court of Canada in R. v. Powley.
4 Editor: For an introduction to the life and contributions of explorer Peter Pond, see the description at http://www.collectionscanada.ca/explorers/h24-1620-e.html. The Peter Pond Society website (www.peterpondsociety.com) maintains a useful bibliography.
5 Editor: Revillon Frères (Brothers Revillon), also known as "The French Company," was a French fur and luxury goods operation that competed with the Hudson's Bay Company from 1903, when the Revillon brothers settled Moosonee, Ontario, until 1936, when the company was bought out by the HBC. Continuing to operate in France, the company eventually merged with the publishing group Les Editions Mondiales in 1982.

REMEMBERING HAROLD CARDINAL

PAUL DEPASQUALE

I hadn't met Harold Cardinal before the "Natives and Settlers Now and Then" conference at the University of Alberta in 2000. Like many, I was familiar with his influential first book, *The Unjust Society*. And I knew from literary texts like Maria Campbell's *Half-Breed* of his influence on many Aboriginal thinkers, including artists, at a time, the early 1970s, when Aboriginal peoples were gathering strength and establishing their voices on many stages, in many formats. This momentum was due in large part to Harold Cardinal. I had taught his essay "A Canadian: What the Hell It's All About," from his second book, *The Rebirth of Canada's Indians*, in the classroom, and continue to teach it today because it's still one of the most effective tools I've found to help students, including those not familiar with Aboriginal histories and cultures, to appreciate the very different conceptions that "Canadians" and Nee-yow or Cree peoples have of their land, nation, and home.

Harold speaks in his writings not just with the intellectual force and eloquence of a highly regarded orator with years of experience and stature; he also speaks with compassion for the hardships of other people in addition to his own, with humility, humour, and a genuine interest in and curiosity about other peoples and traditions, including Western cultures. Through the opportunity to meet him in person and while working with him as he developed his essay for this book, I was also struck by the depth of his appreciation for the spiritual significance of treaty-making, the laws governing human relationships, or what he calls *Wa-koo-to-win*. As I reread his words today, this deep reverence for his people's spiritual traditions resonates powerfully and seems to explain so much of his life's work and accomplishment.

PATRICIA SEED:

If you are very lucky, you may hear someone like Harold Cardinal in your lifetime. I only heard him once, at this conference, but I have never listened to anyone like him before or since. Oratory itself can merely be a learned skill, honed by practised reading from political scripts composed by someone who has marked all the appropriate emotional pauses and inflections. Harold Cardinal did far more than this. He spoke extemporaneously for over an hour, engrossing the entire audience. He combined these extraordinary oratorical skills with acutely phrased observations on comments and points of view (including my own) that he had only heard for the first time five minutes before he spoke. His synthetic and critical intelligence appeared all the more powerful for the modesty with which he spoke—and the obviously heartfelt commitment to his community that lay behind it. I, for one, regret that I will never hear that voice again.

FRANK TOUGH:

My first encounter in person with Harold Cardinal was in 1972 when I heard him speak to a group of students at the University of Manitoba Students' Union Festival of Life and Learning. Years later, when he was associated with the Department of Native Studies at the University of Alberta, I asked him to write a comment for *Native Studies Review* on a recent Supreme Court of Canada decision concerning the effect of the Natural Resources Transfer Agreement (N RTA) on Treaty Rights. This resulted in an interesting discussion, and it has contributed to my obsession with the contrast between history and law as to the meaning of the N RTA.

An apt way to commemorate Dr. Cardinal is to put on the record my introduction to convocation when the University of Alberta awarded Harold an LLD (June 1999). This was his first Honorary degree, and in my view was long overdue. I believe that it is highly appropriate that this recognition came from an Alberta university:

> Eminent Chancellor: On Behalf of the Senate of the University of
> Alberta, I have the privilege to present, for the Honorary Degree
> of a Doctor of Laws, Mr. Harold Cardinal.
> For more than three decades, Harold Cardinal has been an
> articulate and thoughtful leader for the Aboriginal and treaty
> rights movement. At a crucial time in the modern history of
> Indian people, Harold Cardinal provided incisive leadership—
> which in turn has had a profound effect on subsequent relations
> between Aboriginal peoples and the larger society. His analysis

of the federal government's 1969 White Paper on Indian Policy laid a foundation for a very different future for Aboriginal peoples than that proposed by the Department of Indian Affairs. Thirty years ago, the positions advocated by Mr. Cardinal may have seemed extraordinary, but today his analysis has become an accepted and common framework for understanding the historical and contemporary relationships between First Nations and the Canadian government. Canadian society as a whole can thank Harold Cardinal for his reasoned and consistent analysis.

Harold Cardinal's contributions are multifaceted and influential. As an author he published *The Unjust Society* and *The Rebirth of Canada's Indians*. *The Unjust Society* gained influence some thirty years ago by offering a persuasive Indian perspective. As a political leader he served for nine years as President of the Indian Association of Alberta. In his work as a consultant, researcher, and negotiator, he has dealt with the pressing day-to-day problems faced by reserves. As an intellectual, he has been an Assistant Professor, after which he returned to studies, completing an LLB and an LLM. He is currently working on a PhD in Law at the University of British Columbia. He is here with his sons and daughters and his wife Maisie, who is working on a PhD in Education. We wish to offer to you and your family congratulations for this achievement.

Although Mr. Cardinal has lived in Ottawa, Edmonton, and Vancouver and has studied at Harvard, he has remained close to his community of Sucker Creek, Alberta. Harold follows traditional Cree culture, and his comprehension of sacred knowledge is of value to younger Natives. His ability to carry out political and legal discussions between Cree and English is unsurpassed. This expertise at conducting difficult dialogues greatly facilitated the Office of Treaty Commissioner in its most recent work with Saskatchewan Elders. Cardinal speaks easily to both grassroots communities and members of the academy. Although long overdue, this is a good year to honour Mr. Cardinal.

The School of Native Studies is delighted that its mere ten years of existence can be associated with the Senate's honouring of Mr. Cardinal. Without the leadership of people like Harold Cardinal, there would be no Native Studies.

Also this year we acknowledge the Centenary of Treaty Eight, which was signed at Lesser Slave Lake on 21 June 1899. The intention of Indians to enter into a relationship with newcomers is not an obscure fact of history. In official circles today a renewal of treaty relationships has gained recognition, yet this has been a lifelong commitment of Mr. Cardinal.

Eminent Chancellor, it is with the utmost respect that I present to you for the Honorary Degree of a Doctor of Laws a Cree man who has advanced the noble values within Canadian society for the betterment of all First Nations—Mr. Harold Cardinal.

SHARON VENNE:

In the 1960s, Indigenous Peoples were legally allowed to speak for themselves. In the previous years, there had been many laws against movement off the reserves, and against attending meetings or raising money for court actions. These laws were enforced by the state of Canada. Indigenous Peoples went to jail for violating the laws of Canada. Out of this history came Harold Cardinal, supported by his Elders to speak for his people. He spoke unafraid about the injustices heaped on our Peoples. It was a scary time. Indigenous Peoples did not speak out and criticize the government in public. Harold went public and spoke at every opportunity to Indigenous and non-indigenous peoples.

When I was at the University of Victoria in the early 1970s, I went to see Harold speak at the Public Library. Afterwards, he took the time to greet the few Indigenous students and encouraged us to continue with our education because "you are the future warriors for our people." To the end of his life, he was talking about treaties and the way to implement and honour them. In the last year of his life, I spent many hours with him discussing treaties and treaty-making, including the need to write things down for future generations. Harold was concerned that the spiritual significance of treaties was being lost to the younger people. To the end of his human time on the earth, he wanted to find ways to reach out to young people to help them understand their legacy of being the owners and keepers of the land and laws. Harold was a human being for a short time on the earth, but he made valuable contributions that lifted up generations of Indigenous Peoples.

HAROLD CARDINAL (Cree) was President of the Indian Association of
Alberta from 1968 to 1977. His book *The Unjust Society* (Hurtig, 1969;
repr. University of Washington Press, 1999) became one of the most
influential texts on Native rights in Canada. Cardinal was one of the
forces behind "Citizens Plus: A Presentation by the Indian Chiefs of
Alberta to P.E. Trudeau" (1970) (also known as "The Red Paper"), a
response to the assimilationist policies outlined in the Liberal government's White Paper of 1969. His publications include *The Rebirth of
Canadian Indians* (1977) and *The Treaty Elders of Saskatchewan* (2002).
During his distinguished career, he has been the prairie region Vice-
Chief under the Assembly of First Nations, the Alberta Regional
Director of Indian Affairs, Chief of the Sucker Creek First Nation, and
a Treaty 8 negotiator. He received his law degree from the University
of Saskatchewan in 1995, Master of Laws from Harvard University in
1997, and a Doctor of Laws from the University of British Columbia.
The University of Alberta awarded him an honorary doctorate in 1999.
He was the Indigenous Scholar in Residence at the University of
Alberta's Law School and associate professor at the Centre for World
Indigenous Knowledge and Research, Athabasca University, before
passing away on June 3, 2005, at the age of 60.

PAUL W. DEPASQUALE is of Mohawk and European backgrounds and
a member of the Six Nations of the Grand River Territory in Ontario.
He is associate professor of English at the University of Winnipeg
where he teaches courses on Aboriginal literatures and on early-modern European travel and colonialism. DePasquale's recent publications are on subjects such as representations of Aboriginal peoples
in early-modern colonial writings; Cree oral literature; Aboriginal
pedagogy; Iroquois history; and Aboriginal literatures, including
children's literature. He is co-editor of Louis Bird's *Telling our Stories:
Omushkego Voices from Hudson Bay* (Broadview Press, 2005) and co-editor of *Contexts in Canadian Aboriginal and Native American Literatures*
(Broadview Press, forthcoming 2007).

JONATHAN HART, Professor of English and Director of Comparative
Literature at University of Alberta, has held a number of visiting ap-
pointments, most recently at Princeton. His most recent books are

Contesting Empires: Opposition, Promotion, and Slavery (2005) and *Interpreting Cultures: Literature, Religion, and the Human Sciences* (2006).

ERIN MCGREGOR worked as a student researcher for the MatriX project between 2001 and 2005 while earning her Bachelor's degree in Anthropology. In 2005 she worked as an independent contractor and then as an in-house researcher for an Aboriginal law firm in Calgary. In the spring of 2006, she returned to the University of Alberta, where she is presently employed as researcher and research coordinator for the Métis Archival Project.

PATRICIA SEED is professor of history at the University of California, Irvine. An award-winning, highly acclaimed scholar and teacher, her numerous publications include *American Pentimento: The Pursuit of Riches and the Invention of "Indians"* (University of Minnesota Press, 2001); *Ceremonies of Possession in Europe's Conquest of the New World, 1492–1640* (Cambridge University Press, 1995); and *To Love, Honor, and Obey in Colonial Mexico: Conflicts Over Marriage Choice, 1574–1821* (Stanford University Press, 1988). She is currently working on a comparative history of navigation and cartography, especially the history of nautical chart-making.

FRANK TOUGH is professor of Native Studies in the Faculty of Native Studies, University of Alberta, and principal investigator for the Métis Archival Project. He earned his PhD in Geography at York University. His many publications include *As Their Natural Resources Fail: Native People and the Economic History of Northern Manitoba, 1870–1930* (University of British Columbia Press, 1996), awarded the Margaret McWilliams Scholarly Book Medal from the Manitoba Historical Society and the CLIO award from the Canadian Historical Association. Tough has conducted archival research for the Ontario Native Affairs Secretariat, the federal Royal Commission on Aboriginal Peoples, and the Office of the Treaty Commissioner (Saskatchewan). He is the principal investigator of the Métis claim to Northwest Saskatchewan and was awarded a SSHRC grant to conduct a reconstruction of the historical geography of the Métis Nation. For 2005–06, Tough was awarded a McCalla Research Professorship (University of Alberta) for a study entitled "'A course of fraud and forgery and personation': Alberta Métis Respond to the Halfbreed Scrip System, 1910–1926."

SHARON VENNE (Cree) received her law degree from the University of Victoria in 1979 and her Master of Laws from the University of Alberta in 1996. She has done extensive work at the United Nations, playing a key role in helping the UN complete its Study on Treaties in July 1999. In December 2003, Sharon was invited by the United Nations as an expert to participate in a seminar on the follow-up to the Treaty Study. Her many articles and books include *Our Elders Understand Our Rights: Evolving International Law Regarding Indigenous Peoples* (Theytus, 1998; second printing 2003) and *Islands in Captivity: The International Tribunal on the Rights of Indigenous Hawaiians* (South End Press, 2005), which Venne co-edited with Ward Churchill. Sharon has lectured on the rights of Indigenous Peoples at universities in the United States, Canada, France, Australia, and New Zealand. She has received numerous awards for her work on the rights of Indigenous Peoples. At present, Sharon is working with the Akaitcho Dene to implement their Treaty negotiated and concluded in 1900 in Deninu Kue, Akaitcho Territory.

Aboriginal People in Manitoba. Her Majesty the Queen in Right of Canada, 2002.

"Aboriginal Schooling." Editorial. *Winnipeg Free Press.* 18 June 2004: A14.

Aboriginal Task Group. *Eagle's Eye View: An Environmental Scan of the Aboriginal Community in Winnipeg.* Winnipeg, MB: United Way of Canada, 2004.

Alaska Native Claims Settlement Act. Congress. 92nd. H.R. 10361971: 1601–42.

Australia. *Commonwealth Consolidated Acts.* Native Title Act 1993 sec. 223.

Barron, F. Laurie, and Joseph Garcea, eds. *Urban Reserves: Forging New Relationships in Saskatchewan.* Saskatoon, SA: Purich Publishing, 1999.

Battiste, Marie, ed. *Reclaiming Indigenous Voice and Vision.* Vancouver, BC: UBC Press, 2000.

Biker, Julio Firmino Judice, ed. *Coleção De Tratados e Concertos de Pazes que o Estado da Índia Portuguesa Fez com os Reis e Senhores com quem teve Relações nas Partes da Ásia e África Oriental desde o Principio da Conquista ate ao Fim do Século XVIII.* 14 vols. Lisbon: Imprensa Nacional, 1881–1887.

Bird, Louis. Interview with Paul DePasquale. Audiocassette recorded 20 March 2004.

Bird, Louis. *Telling Our Stories: Omushkego Legends and Histories from Hudson Bay.* Eds. Jennifer S.H. Brown, Paul W. DePasquale, and Mark F. Ruml. Peterborough, ON: Broadview Press, 2005.

Black, Henry Campbell. *Black's Law Dictionary: Definitions of the Terms and Phrases of American and English Jurisprudence, Ancient and Modern.* Abr. 5th ed. St. Paul: West Publishing, 1983.

Blackstone, William. *Commentaries on the Laws of England.* Vol. 2. 4 vols, 1753–1766. Oxford: Clarendon Press, 1966.

"Board Tells School to Pick Team Name." *Winnipeg Free Press.* 11 May 2004: A4.

Burgess, Olive. "Special Rights Aren't Democratic." Letter. *Winnipeg Free Press.* 4 Feb. 2004: A11.

Bussidor, Ila, and Üstün Bilgen-Reinart. *Night Spirits: The Story of the Relocation of the Sayisi Dene.* Winnipeg, MB: University of Manitoba Press, 1997.

Canada. *Treaty No. 10 and Reports of Commissioners.* Ottawa: Roger Duhamel, Queen's Printer and Controller of Stationery, 1966.

Canada. *Debates of the Senate: 1922.* Ottawa: F.A. Acland, Printer to the King's Most Excellent Majesty, 1922.

Canada. *Report of the Royal Commission on Aboriginal Peoples: Perspectives and Realities.* Vol. 4. Ottawa: Minister of Supply and Services Canada, 1996.

Canada. *Debates of the Senate of the Dominion of Canada: 1921.* Ottawa: Thomas Mulvey, Printer to the King's Most Excellent Majesty, 1921.

Cobell v. Kempthorne (June 10, 1996–present) <http://www.indiantrust.com/>.

"Consideration of Reports Submitted by States Parties under Article 9 of the Convention." *Committee on the Elimination of Racial Discrimination.* 61st ed. New York: United Nations, 2002.

Delgamuukw v. British Columbia. 3 S.C.R. Supreme Court (Canada) 1997.

Deloria, Vine, and David E. Wilkins. *Tribes, Treaties, and Constitutional Tribulations.* Austin, TX: University of Texas Press, 2000.

DePasquale, Paul W. "'Worth the Noting': Aboriginal Agency and European Ambivalence in Meta Incognita, 1576–1578." Eds. Jennifer Brown and Elizabeth Vibert. *Reading Beyond Words: Contexts for Native History.* 2nd ed. Peterborough, ON: Broadview Press, 2003. 5–38.

DePasquale, Paul W. "Recognize Spirit of Treaties." Letter. *Winnipeg Free Press.* 4 Nov. 2003.

DePasquale, Paul W. "Re-Writing the Virginian Paradise: The Conflicted Author(s) of a Late Sixteenth-Century Travel Account." Eds. Glenn Burger et al. *Making Contact: Maps, Identity, and Travel.* Edmonton, AB: University of Alberta Press, 2003. 143–72.

Diario De Sesiones Del Senado, Legislatura 339ª, Extraordinaria Sesión 22ª. Senado de Chile. 9 marzo 1999.

Donald, Dwayne Trevor. "Edmonton Pentimento: Re-Reading History in the Case of Papaschase Cree." *Journal of Canadian Curriculum Studies.* 1.1 (Spring 2004): 21–55.

Elias, Peter Douglas. *The Dakota of the Canadian Northwest: Lessons for Survival.* Winnipeg, MB: University of Manitoba Press, 1988.

Ens, Gerhard J. *Homeland to Hinterland: The Changing World of the Red River Metis in the Nineteenth Century.* Toronto: University of Toronto Press, 1996.

Ens, Gerhard J. "Dispossession or Adaptation? Migration and Persistence of the Red River Metis, 1835–1890." *Canadian Historical Association Papers* (1988): 120–44.

Flanagan, Thomas, and Gerhard Ens. "Metis Land Grants in Manitoba: A Statistical Summary." *Histoire Sociale/Social History* 27 (1994): 65–87.

Flanagan, Thomas. "The Market for Métis Lands in Manitoba: An Exploratory Study." *Prairie Forum* 16.1 (1991): 1–20.

Flanagan, Thomas. "Comment on Ken Hatt, 'The North-West Rebellion Scrip Commissions, 1885–1889'." *1885 and After: Native Society in Transition.* Eds. F.L. Barron and J.B. Waldram. Regina: Canadian Plains Research Center, 1986. 205–09.

Fleras, Augie, and Jean Leonard Elliott. *The Nations Within: Aboriginal-State Relations in Canada, the United States, and New Zealand.* Don Mills: Oxford University Press, 1992.

Francis, Daniel. *The Imaginary Indian: The Image of the Indian in Canadian Culture.* Vancouver, BC: Arsenal Pulp Press, 1992.

Friesen, Jean. "Magnificent Gifts: The Treaties of Canada with the Indians of the Northwest, 1869–1876." Price 203–13.

Goyette, Linda. "Land Grab: The X files." *Canadian Geographic* 123.2 (March/April 2003): 70–80.

Hakluyt, Richard. *The Principal Navigations, Voyages, Traffiques and Discoveries of the English Nation Made by Sea or over-Land to the Remote and Farthest Distant Quarters of the Earth at Any Time within the Compasse of These 1600 Yeeres.* Vol. 8. Glasgow: J. MacLehose and Sons, 1903–05.

Hall, Anthony J. *The American Empire and the Fourth World.* Montreal and Kingston: McGill–Queen's University Press, 2003.

Hall, D.J. "The Half-Breed Claims Commission." *Alberta History* 25.2 (1977): 1–8.

Hall, Stuart. *Representations: Cultural Representations and Signifying Practices.* London: Sage Publications, 1997.

Hall, Stuart. "Representations and the Media." Dir. Sut Jhally. Media Education Foundation, 1997.

Hallam, Elizabeth and Brian V. Street. Introduction. *Cultural Encounters: Representing 'Otherness'.* London and New York: Routledge, 2000. 1–10.

Hatt, Ken. "The Northwest Scrip Commissions as Federal Policy: Some Initial Findings." *Canadian Journal of Native Studies* 3.1 (1983): 117–29.

Hatt, Ken. "North-West Rebellion Scrip Commissions, 1885–1889." *1885 and After: Native Society in Transition.* Eds. F.L. Barron and J.B. Waldram. Regina: Canadian Plains Research Center, 1986. 189–204.

Holdsworth, William Searle. *An Historical Introduction to the Land Law.* Oxford: Clarendon Press, 1927.

Hough, Franklin B., ed. *Proceedings of the Commissioners of Indian Affairs.* Vol. 1. Albany, 1861.

Imai, Shin. *Aboriginal Law Handbook.* 2nd ed. Scarborough, ON: Carswell, 1999.

Innis, Harold A. *The Fur Trade In Canada: An Introduction to Canadian Economic History.* 1930. Toronto: University of Toronto Press, 1999.

Kawharu, Hugh, ed. *Waitangi: Maori and Pakeha Perspectives.* Auckland: Oxford University Press, 1989.

Kent, Donald H. *History of Pennsylvania Purchases from the Indians.* New York: Garland Pub. Inc, 1974.

Lambrecht, Kirk N. *The Administration of Dominion Lands, 1870–1930.* Regina: Canadian Plains Research Center, 1991.

Lawrenchuk, Michael. *As Long as the Sun Shines.* Produced by the Assembly of Manitoba Chiefs, 1999.

"A Liberal Contribution." Editorial. *Winnipeg Free Press.* 9 July 2004. A10.

Littlefield, Alice, and Martha C. Knack, eds. *Native Americans and Wage Labor: Ethnohistorical Perspectives.* Norman, OK.: University of Oklahoma Press, 1996.

Long, John. "Who Got What at Winisk, Treaty-making, 1930." *The Beaver* 75.1 (1995): 23–31.

Lyons, Oren, ed. *Exiled in the Land of the Free: Democracy, Indian Nations, and the U.S. Constitution.* Sante Fe: Clear Light Publishers, 1992.

Maaka, Roger, and Augie Fleras. "Re-constitutionalising Treaty Works: The Waitangi Tribunal." Unpublished paper. Christchurch: University of Canterbury, 1998.

Mabo v. Queensland. 175 Commonwealth Law Reports 109. High Court Australia, 1992.

MacDonald, K.M. "Commercial Implications of Native Title for Mining and Resources." *Commercial Implications of Native Title.* Eds. Bryan Horrigan and Simon Young. Leichardt, NSW: The Federation Press, 1997. 114–125.

MacDougall, Brenda. "Socio-Cultural Development and Identity Formation of Métis Communities in Northwestern Saskatchewan, 1776–1907." Diss. University of Saskatchewan, 2005.

MacLennan, Kevin. "For the 'Purposes of the Dominion': Métis Entitlement and the Regulatory Regime of 'Halfbreed' Scrip.'" Honours Thesis. School of Native Studies, University of Alberta, 2002.

Mailhot, P.R., and D.N. Sprague. "Persistent Settlers: The Dispersal and Resettlement of the Red River Metis, 1870–1885." *Canadian Ethnic Studies* 17.2 (1985): 1–30.

Mainville, Robert. *An Overview of Aboriginal and Treaty Rights and Compensation For Their Breach.* Saskatoon, SA: Purich Publishing, 2001.

Marcos, Subcomandante. *Viento Primero.* Selva Lacandona, 1992.

Mather, Cotton. *Fair Weather.* Boston, 1692.

"Mayor Defends Reserves." *Winnipeg Free Press.* 10 Sept. 2003

"Mayor Will Fight for Urban Reserves." *Winnipeg Free Press.* 7 Sept. 2003.

McLoughlin, William. *After the Trail of Tears: The Cherokees' Struggle for Sovereignty, 1839–1880.* Chapel Hill: University of North Carolina Press, 1993.

Milsom, S.F.C. *Historical Foundations of the Common Law.* 2nd ed. London: Butterworths, 1981.

"Morden School to Drop Mohawks Name." *Winnipeg Free Press.* 18 Mar. 2004: A1.

"Morden Trustee to Vote No to Mohawks Name Change." *Winnipeg Free Press.* 26 Mar. 2004: A10.

"Morden's Mohawks are History." *Winnipeg Free Press.* 12 Apr. 2005.

More, Thomas. 1515. *Utopia.* Eds. G. Logan and R. Adams. Cambridge: Cambridge University Press, 1995.

Morris, Alexander. *The Treaties of Canada with the Indians of Manitoba and the North West, Including the Negotiations on Which They Were Based.* 1880. Calgary, AB: Fifth House, 1991.

Morton, Nathaniel. *New England's Memoriall.* Cambridge [Mass.]: Printed by S.G. and M.J. for John Vsher of Boston, 1669.

Murray, Glen. "Treaty is a Treaty, Deal is a Deal." *Winnipeg Free Press.* 18 Sept. 2003: A13.

Nelson, Melissa. "Becoming Métis." *At Home on the Earth: Becoming Native to Our Place. A Multicultural Anthology*. Ed. David Landis Barnhill. Berkeley, CA: University of California Press, 1999. 113–18.

New Zealand, Waitangi Tribunal. *Muriwhenua Fishing Report*. Wai 22. Wellington: Department of Justice, 1988.

New Zealand, Waitangi Tribunal. *Ngai Tahu Seas Fisheries Report*. Wellington: Brooker & Friend Ltd, 1992.

New Zealand, Waitangi Tribunal. *The Whanganui River Report*. Wellington: GP Publications, 1999.

O'Brien, David. "Study Points to Trouble in Aboriginal Housing." *Winnipeg Free Press*. 25 May 2004: B7.

Orange, Claudia. *The Treaty of Waitangi*. Wellington: Allen and Unwin, 1987.

The Oxford English Dictionary. 2nd ed. 1985.

Pocock, J.G.A. "Law, Sovereignty and History in a Divided Culture: The Case of New Zealand and the Treaty of Waitangi." *McGill Law Journal* 43 (1998): 481–506.

Pocock, J.G.A. *The Discovery of Islands: Essays in British History*. New York: Cambridge University Press, 2005.

Price, Richard T. Introduction. Price ix–xviii.

Price, Richard T., ed. *The Spirit of the Alberta Indian Treaties*. Institute for Research on Public Policy, 1979. Edmonton, AB: University of Alberta Press, 1999.

"Public Forum Eases Urban Reserve Fears." *Winnipeg Free Press*. 24 Sept. 2003: A3.

Quinn, David B. "Renaissance Influences in English Colonization." *Transactions of the Royal Historical Society* 5th ser., 27 (1976): 73–92.

Rabson, Mia. "Housing Crisis Ignored, Chiefs Say." *Winnipeg Free Press*. 27 Jan. 2005: B6.

Rasmussen, William M.S., and Robert S. Tilton. *Pocohontas: Her Life & Legend*. Richmond, VA.: Virginia Historical Society, 1994.

Ray, Arthur J. "Aboriginal Title and Treaty Rights Research: A Comparative Look at Australia, Canada, New Zealand and the United States." *New Zealand Journal of History* 37.1 (2003): 5–21.

Ray, Arthur J. "Native History on Trial: Confessions of an Expert Witness." *Canadian Historical Review* 84.2 (2003): 253–273.

"Reserve Judgment." Editorial. *Winnipeg Free Press*. 11 Sept. 2003: A12.

Richtik, James M. "The Policy Framework for Settling the Canadian West, 1870–1880." *Agricultural History* 49 (1975): 613–628.

Richtik, James M. "Competition for Settlers, The Canadian Viewpoint." *Great Plains Quarterly* 3.1 (1983): 39–49.

Rountree, Helen C. *Pocahontas's People: The Powhatan Indians of Virginia Through Four Centuries*. Norman: University of Oklahoma Press, 1990.

Rountree, Helen C. *The Powhatan Indians of Virginia: Their Traditional Culture*. Norman: University of Oklahoma Press, 1989.

Sanders, Carol. "Urban Reserves: What Are They, and How Do They Work?" *Winnipeg Free Press*. 14 Sept. 2003: B1.

Sawchuk, Joe, Patricia Sawchuk, and Theresa Ferguson. *Metis Land Rights in Alberta: A Political History*. Edmonton: Metis Association of Alberta, 1981.

Schulte-Tenckhoff, Isabelle. "Reassessing the Paradigm of Domestication: The Problematic of Indigenous Treaties." *Review of Constitutional Studies*. 4.2 (1997): 239–89.

Schulz, Herb. "Urban Reserves a Tax Dodge." Letter. *Winnipeg Free Press*. 2 Oct. 2006: A10.

"Scrip." *Gage Canadian Concise Dictionary*. Toronto: Gage Educational Publishing, 2002. 772.

Seaborne, A.A. "A Population Geography of North Saskatchewan," *Musk-Ox* 12 (1973): 49–57.

Seed, Patricia. *American Pentimento: The Invention of Indians and the Pursuit of Riches*. Minneapolis: University of Minnesota Press, 2001.

Sharp, Andrew. *Justice and the Maori: The Philosophy and Practice of Maori Claims in New Zealand since the 1970s.* 2nd ed. Auckland: Oxford University Press,1997.

Simpson, S. Rowton. "Government Lawlessness in the Administration of Manitoba Land Claims, 1870–1887." *Manitoba Law Journal* 10.4 (1980): 415–441.

Simpson, S. Rowton. *Land Law and Registration.* Cambridge: Cambridge University Press, 1976.

Sinclair, Vincent. "Posturing Just Stalls Reserve Talks." *Winnipeg Free Press.* 26 Sept. 2003.

Skerritt, Jen. "Natives to Protest Cutbacks in Federal Health Programs." *Winnipeg Free Press.* 27 Sept. 2006: A8.

Slattery, Brian, and Linda Charlton, eds. *Canadian Native Law Cases: 1911–1930.* Vol. 4. Saskatoon: Native Law Centre, University of Saskatchewan, 1986.

Sprague, D.N. "The Manitoba Land Question, 1870–1882." *Journal of Canadian Studies* 15.3 (1980): 74–84.

Stephenson, M.A. "Negotiating Resource Development Agreements with Indigenous People: Comparative International Lessons." *Commercial Implications of Native Title.* Eds. Bryan Horrigan and Simon Young. Leichardt, NSW: The Federation Press, 1997. 240–319.

Stonechild, Blair, and Bill Waiser. *Loyal Till Death: Indians and the North-West Rebellion.* Calgary, AB: Fifth House, 1997.

The Supreme Court of Canada Decision on Aboriginal Title: Delgamuukw. Foreword, Don Ryan. Commentary, Stan Persky. Vancouver: Greystone Books and David Suzuki Foundation, 1998.

Tanner, Adrian, ed. *The Politics of Indianness: Case Studies of Native Ethnopolitics in Canada.* St. Johns, Newfoundland: Institute of Social and Economic Research, 1983.

Taylor, John Leonard. "Canada's Northwest Indian Policy in the 1870s: Traditional Premises and Necessary Innovations." Price 3–7.

Tee-Hit-Ton Indians v U.S. 348 United States Reports 272. Supreme Court 1955.

"This Land is My Land." *The Economist.* 14 Sept. 2006. Available at http://www.economist.com/world/la/displaystory.cfm?story_id=7911293.

Tough, Frank, and Leah Dorion. "'The Claims of the Halfbreeds...Have Been Finally Closed': A Study of Treaty Ten and Treaty Five Adhesion Scrip." *A Research Report for the Royal Commission on Aboriginal Peoples.* 1993. In: Government of Canada. *Royal Commission on Aboriginal Peoples, For Seven Generations: An Information Legacy of the Royal Commission on Aboriginal Peoples.* [CD ROM] Ottawa: Libraxus Inc., 1997. 46–50.

Tough, Frank. "Activities of Metis Scrip Commissions." *Atlas of Saskatchewan.* Ed. Ka-iu Fung. Saskatoon: University of Saskatchewan, 1999. 61–62.

Tough, Frank. "Aboriginal Rights Versus The Deed Of Surrender: The Legal Rights of Native Peoples and Canada's Acquisition of the Hudson's Bay Company Territory." *Prairie Forum.* 17.2 (1992): 225–50.

Tough, Frank. *"As Their Natural Resources Fail": Native Peoples and the Economic History of Northern Manitoba, 1870–1930.* Vancouver: University of British Columbia Press, 1996.

US Commission on Civil Rights. *Indian Tribes: A Continuing Quest for Survival.* Washington, D.C.: US Government Printing Office, 1981.

Uchtmann, Robert H. "Treaties Clearly Gave up Land." Letter. *Winnipeg Free Press.* 24 Oct. 2003.

United States v. Dann. 470 United States Report 39. United States Supreme Court, 1985.

United States v. Dann. 493 United States Reports 890 1989.

United States v. Dann. 873, Federal Reports 2d, 1189. 9th Cir 1989.

"Urban Natives Scoff at Treaty." *Winnipeg Free Press.* 2 June 2004: A6.

"Urban Reserves Will Happen: Deputy Mayor." *Winnipeg Free Press.* 31 Jan. 2004: A5.

Usher, Peter J. "Aboriginal Property Systems in Land and Resources." *Indigenous Land Rights in Commonwealth Countries.* Eds. Garth Cant, John Overton, and Eric Pawson. Christchurch: Canterbury University Press, 1993. 38–44.

Usher, Peter J., Frank Tough, and Robert M. Galois. "Reclaiming the Land: Aboriginal Title, Treaty Rights and Land Claims in Canada." *Applied Geography* 12 (1992): 109–32.

Venne, Sharon H., ed. "Treaty Doubletalk in Canada." *Indigenous Law Bulletin: Indigenous Perspectives on Law & Rights* 5.1 (2000): 8–11.

Venne, Sharon H., ed. "Understanding Treaty Six: An Indigenous Perspective." *Aboriginal and Treaty Rights in Canada.* Ed. M. Asch. Vancouver: University of British Columbia Press, 1997.

Venne, Sharon H., ed. *Our Elders Understand our Rights: Evolving International Law Regarding Indigenous Peoples.* Penticton, BC: Theytus Books, 1998.

Venne, Sharon H., ed. *Honour Bound: Onion Lake and the Spirit of Treaty Six—The International Validity of Treaties with Indigenous Peoples.* Copenhagen: IWGIA Document No. 84, 1997.

Walker, Ranginui. "Maori Sovereignty: The Maori Perspective." *Maori Sovereignty: The Maori Perspective.* Ed. Hineani Melbourne. Auckland: Hodder Moa Beckett Publishers Limited, 1995.

Washburn, Wilcomb. *Red Man's Land, White Man's Law.* New York: Charles Scribner's Sons, 1971.

Washburn, Wilcomb. "The Moral and Legal Justification for Dispossessing the Indians." *Seventeenth-Century America: Essays in Colonial History.* Ed. James Morton Smith. Chapel Hill, NC: University of North Carolina Press, 1959. 15–32.

Williams, Roger. "A Key into the Language." *Complete Writings.* (1643). Vol. 1. New York: Russell & Russell, 1963.

Index

Canada (*continued*)
assimilation policies, 8–10, 67–69
deconstruction of knowledge, 72–76
discovery doctrine, 87
dispossession of Aboriginal peoples, ix
hereditary systems, 76
identity issues, 66–67, 86
mapping systems, 96, 97n2
as postcolonial society, 66–70
repatriation of BNA Act, xxx
See also Canada, treaties in; Métis scrip
Canada, treaties in
Aboriginal title, xxv, 28–29, 58n3
Constitution and, xxv, xxxiin 9, 12, 24,
28–29, 71–72, 76
land ownership systems and, xxix,
17–23, 96, 99
legal history of, 8–14, 67–69
modern treaties, 84–85, 88–89
natural resources, 26–27
surveying for, 56
treaty commissioners, 4–9
UN recognition and review of, 10–13,
82–83
use of English language in, 23, 72–73
violations and alterations, 24, 83
See also treaties, numbered
Canadian Museum for Human Rights,
Winnipeg, xxxin2
capitalism and Aboriginal peoples, 29–31
Cardinal, Harold
assessing his impact, x, xiv, 99–102
biographical notes on, xv, 73–74, 77n1,
103
claims commission recommendations,
xxvii
on nation-building, x, xxx, 65–77
on post-secondary education, 87,
94–96
works, 99, 101
Catholic Church, 15n8, 83–84
Ceremonies of Possession (Seed), 93, 104
Charter of Rights and Freedoms, 70–72,
77n6–7
Cherokee, 19–20, 83, 88–89
Chiapas, Mexico, 30
Chile, 12–13, 31
Chrétien, Jean, xxiv, 8, 10
Christianity
Aboriginal peoples and, 67–69, 92–94
Garden of Eden and Great Turtle Island,
3–4
land ownership and, xxiv, 83–84

Churchill, Manitoba, xxxiin16
Cobell v. Kempthorne, 27
collective rights, 70, 72
colonialism
colonization, as term, 66–67
features of, xxiii–xxiv, 87
internalization by Aboriginals, 65–69,
87
treaties and land ownership under, xxiv,
17–20
views of Aboriginal peoples, xvii–xviii,
xxi–xxxiii, 83, 88
See also land ownership systems
Columbia, 30
Columbus, Christopher, xvii, xxiii
conference, "Natives and Settlers Now
and Then" (2000), Edmonton,
Alberta, xv–xvi, xxx–xxxi
Constitution Act of 1982, xxv, xxxiin12, 9,
24, 28–29, 71–72, 76
Creation, as term, 14n2
Creation, treaty-making and, 1–2, 7–8,
14, 81–82
Cree language, 86, 87
Cree people. *See* Nihiyow, Cree people
Criminal Code, land titles fraud, 54–55,
57
Cross Lake, Manitoba, xxxin5
Crown Land, as term, 5

Dakota, xxxin7
Dann v. U.S., 25, 32n4
deconstruction of colonial discourse,
72–73, 76
Delgamuukw v. British Columbia, xxv, 29,
58n3, 94
Dene, xxvi, xxviii, xxxiin16, 2–3, 34–35
Department of Interior, Métis scrip
processing, 38–43, 46–48, 51
DePasquale, Paul
biographical notes on, xv, 103
on colonial past in the present, xv–xxxiii
on Harold Cardinal, 99
Dickason, Olive, viii
discovery, as term, 3–4, 87
diseases, introduction of, 90
domestic treaties, as term, 10
dominate, as term, 67–69
Dominion Land Offices, 39–43, 47–48,
52–53, 55
Dominion Lands Act, 39, 55, 63n66
Donald, Dwayne T., 14n4
Dutch, treaty making, 20–21, 93